TExES

Mathematics 7-12 Practice Questions

Mometrix

TEST PREPARATION

DEAR FUTURE EXAM SUCCESS STORY

First of all, **THANK YOU** for purchasing Mometrix study materials!

Second, congratulations! You are one of the few determined test-takers who are committed to doing whatever it takes to excel on your exam. **You have come to the right place.** We developed these practice tests with one goal in mind: to deliver you the best possible approximation of the questions you will see on test day.

Standardized testing is one of the biggest obstacles on your road to success, which only increases the importance of doing well in the high-pressure, high-stakes environment of test day. Your results on this test could have a significant impact on your future, and these practice tests will give you the repetitions you need to build your familiarity and confidence with the test content and format to help you achieve your full potential on test day.

Your success is our success

We would love to hear from you! If you would like to share the story of your exam success or if you have any questions or comments in regard to our products, please contact us at **800-673-8175** or **support@mometrix.com**.

Thanks again for your business and we wish you continued success!

Sincerely,
The Mometrix Test Preparation Team

Table of Contents

Practice Test #1

1. Which of the following expressions gives the area A of the triangle below as a function of sides a and b?

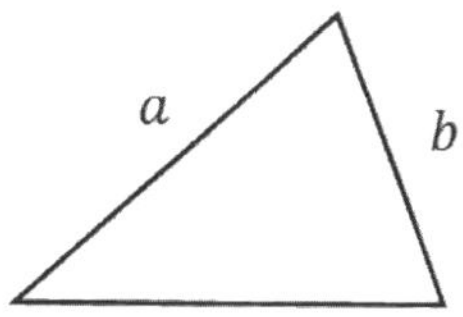

a. $\frac{2a^2-b^2}{4}$
b. $\frac{ab-a^2}{2}$
c. $\frac{b\sqrt{a^2-b^2}}{2}$
d. $\frac{b\sqrt{4a^2-b^2}}{4}$

2. Which of these does NOT simulate randomly selecting a student from a group of 11 students?

a. Assigning each student a unique card value of A, 2, 3, 4, 5, 6, 7, 8, 9, 10, or J, removing queens and kings from a standard deck of 52 cards, shuffling the remaining cards, and drawing a single card from the deck
b. Assigning each student a unique number 0–10 and using a computer to randomly generate a number within that range
c. Assigning each student a unique number from 2 to 12, rolling two dice, and finding the sum of the numbers on the dice
d. All of these can be used as a simulation of the event.

3. A mountain climber climbs through rough terrain. She climbs 480 feet, 610 feet, 295 feet, and 303 feet over a period of 4 days. Estimate the distance she climbs over the four-day period to the nearest hundred feet.

a. 1,500 feet
b. 1,600 feet
c. 1,700 feet
d. 1,800 feet

4. Which of these is the least biased sampling technique?

a. A PE teacher records the height of the entire girls' volleyball team to show that the average height of high school girls today is greater than it was 50 years ago.
b. A woman surveys her entire neighborhood for opinions on the new business coming to town.
c. A news website requests feedback via an anonymous online form.
d. A journalist calls the first 50 names on a randomly generated list of all voters in the county to request opinions on a politician.

5. Mr. Abbas is teaching a lesson on calculating perimeter and area of two-dimensional shapes. He wants the lesson to engage his students in the practice of using appropriate tools strategically. Which of the following activities is best aligned with Mr. Abbas' objective?

a. Give each student a piece of yarn, a ruler, and a worksheet with pictures of various shapes. Ask students to use the tools to determine the perimeters and areas of the shapes.
b. Give each student a worksheet with pictures of various objects. Ask them to calculate the perimeter and area, showing their work.
c. Give each student a ruler or yardstick and a worksheet naming various objects in the classroom. Ask students to find the area of those objects.
d. Give each student a set of interlocking cubes and a worksheet naming various objects in the classroom. Ask students to estimate the area of those objects.

6. Which of the following could be the graph of $y = a(x+b)^2(x+c)^2$ if $a > 0$?

a.

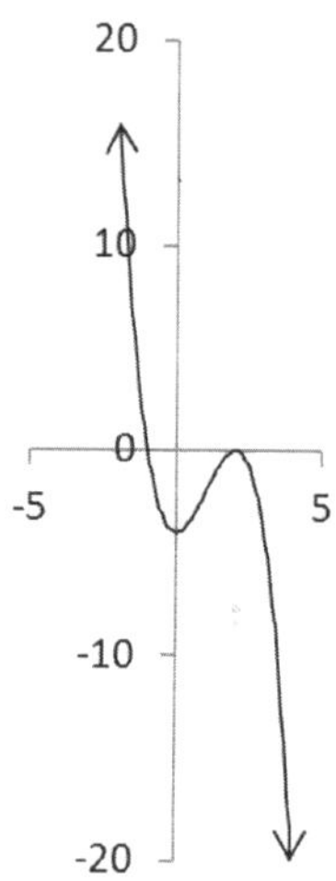

b.

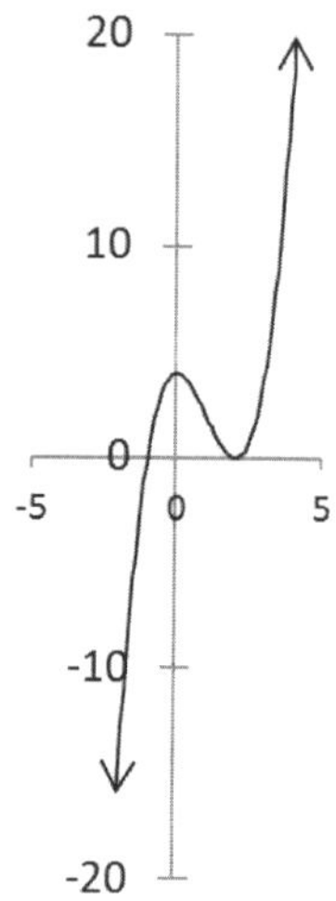

c.

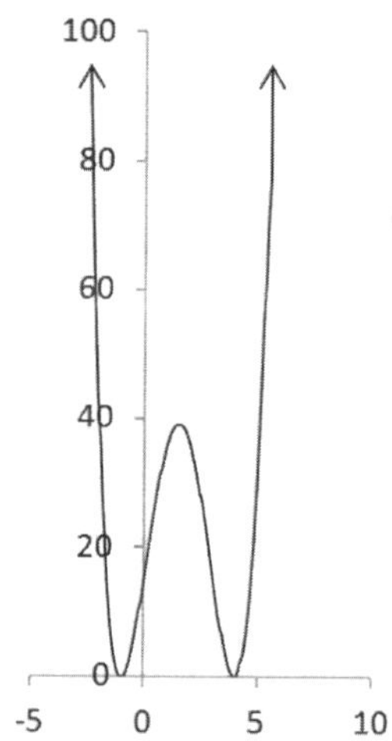

d.

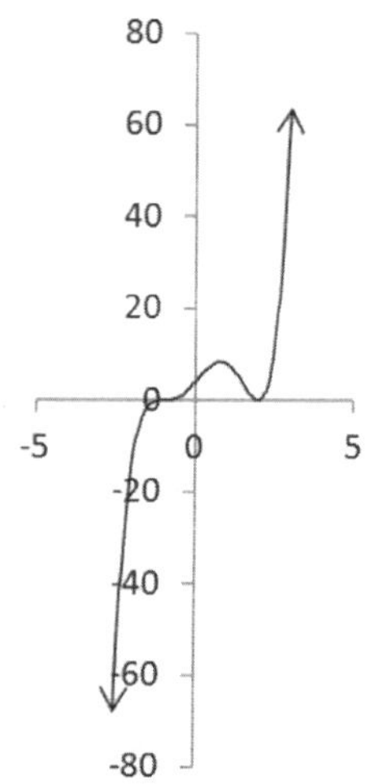

7. A shirt is marked down by 25% and placed on a clearance rack, on which is posted a sign reading, "Take an extra 30% off already reduced merchandise." What fraction of the original price is the final sale price of the shirt?

a. $\frac{9}{20}$
b. $\frac{11}{20}$
c. $\frac{21}{40}$
d. $\frac{7}{10}$

8. If $\sin\theta = \frac{\sqrt{3}}{2}$ when $\frac{\pi}{2} < \theta < \pi$, what is the value of θ?

a. $\frac{\pi}{6}$
b. $\frac{3\pi}{4}$
c. $\frac{2\pi}{3}$
d. $\frac{5\pi}{6}$

9. If the square of twice the sum of x and three is equal to the product of twenty-four and x, which of these is a possible value of x?

a. $6+3\sqrt{2}$
b. $\frac{3}{2}$
c. $-3i$
d. -3

10. When a teacher explains that the order of the addends or factors does not affect the sum or product, he is teaching a lesson about:

a. Comparing and ordering fractions
b. The properties of real numbers
c. Using ratios and proportions
d. Inductive reasoning

11. To which of the following sets of numbers does $\frac{1}{4}$ belong?

a. The set of real numbers
b. The set of irrational numbers
c. The set of integers
d. The set of whole numbers

12. Simplify $\sqrt{\frac{-32x^4}{75y^5}}$.

a. $\frac{2x^2i\sqrt{2y}}{9y^3}$
b. $\frac{4x^2i\sqrt{6y}}{15y^3}$
c. $\frac{-2x^2\sqrt{21y}}{9y^3}$
d. $\frac{8x^3i\sqrt{6y}}{27y^2}$

13. Which of the following fractions is closest to $\frac{15{,}012}{19{,}938}$?

a. $\frac{1}{4}$
b. $\frac{3}{4}$
c. $\frac{4}{5}$
d. $\frac{5}{9}$

14. A car is driving along the highway at a constant speed when it runs over a pebble, which becomes lodged in one of the tire's treads. If this graph represents the height h of the pebble above the road in inches (y-axis) as a function of time t in seconds (x-axis), which of these statements is true?

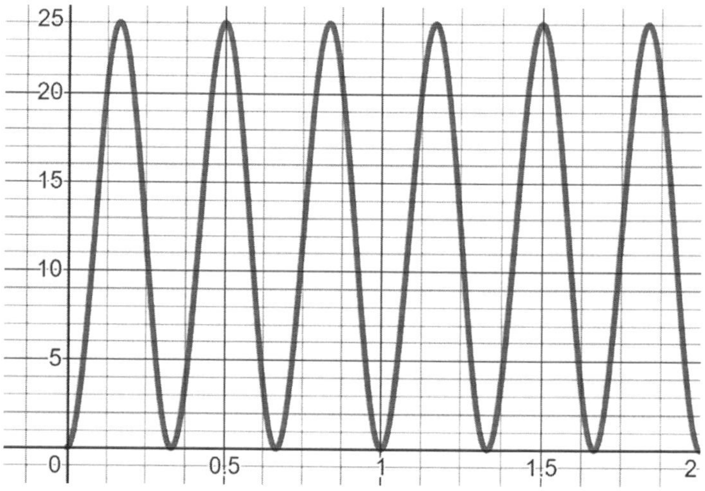

a. The outer diameter of the tire is 12 inches, and the tire rotates 60 times per minute.
b. The outer diameter of the tire is 24 inches, and the tire rotates 60 times per minute.
c. The outer diameter of the tire is 12 inches, and the tire rotates 180 times per minute.
d. The outer diameter of the tire is 24 inches, and the tire rotates 180 times per minute.

15. Starting at his house, Juan walks $(x - 10)$ meters west and x meters south to get to the park. On a neighborhood map that has a scale of 1 cm : 20 m, the straight-line distance between Juan's house and the park is 2.5 cm. How far did Juan walk to the park?

a. 30 m
b. 40 m
c. 50 m
d. 70 m

16. On a floor plan drawn at a scale of $1:150$, the area of a rectangular room is 20 cm^2. What is the actual area of the room?

a. 4,500 cm^2
b. 45,000 cm^2
c. 45 m^2
d. 450 m^2

17. A weight suspended on a spring is at its equilibrium point 6 inches above the top of a table. When the weight is pulled down 1.5 inches, it bounces above the equilibrium point and returns to the point from which it was released in 0.5 seconds. Which of these can be used to model the weight's height h above the table as a function of time t in seconds?

a. $h = -1.5\sin(2\pi t) + 6$
b. $h = -3\cos(\pi t) + 4.5$
c. $h = -1.5\cos(4\pi t) + 6$
d. $h = -3\cos(0.5\pi t) + 4.5$

18. Simplify $(3 - 2i)^2 + (7 + 7i)$.

a. $\sqrt{119}$
b. $12 - 5i$
c. $12 + 5i$
d. 13

19. A circle is inscribed inside quadrilateral $ABCD$. $\overline{CD}$ is bisected by the point at which it is tangent to the circle. If $\overline{AB} = 10$, $\overline{BC} = 12$, and $\overline{CD} = 8$, then what is the length of $\overline{AD}$?

a. $\overline{AD} = 11$
b. $\overline{AD} = 7.5$
c. $\overline{AD} = 6$
d. $\overline{AD} = 2\sqrt{11}$

20. Solve $x^4 + 64 = 20x^2$.

a. $x = \{2, 4\}$
b. $x = \{-4, -2, 2, 4\}$
c. $x = \{2i, 4i\}$
d. $x = \{-4i, -2i, 2i, 4i\}$

21. Which of the following expressions gives the area A of the triangle below in terms of x? Note: The figure is not drawn to scale.

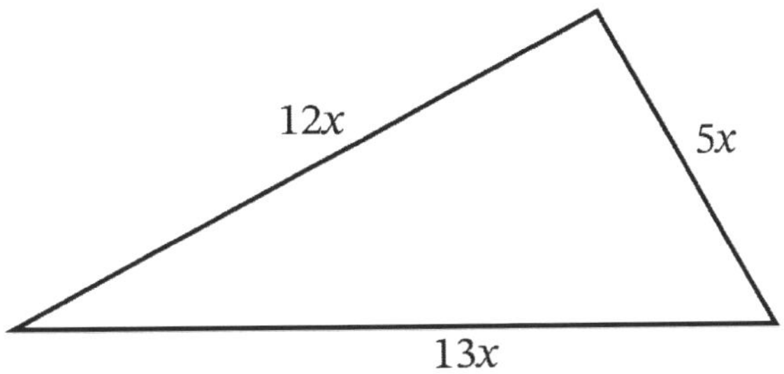

a. $30x^2$
b. $5\sqrt{3x^2 - 1}$
c. $\frac{x\sqrt{5x^2}}{12}$
d. $\frac{3x\sqrt{13x^2}}{25}$

22. Given statements p and q, which of the following is the truth table for the statement:

$$q \leftrightarrow \neg(p \wedge q)$$

a.

p	q	$q \leftrightarrow \neg(p \wedge q)$
T	T	F
T	F	T
F	T	T
F	F	T

b.

p	q	$q \leftrightarrow \neg(p \wedge q)$
T	T	T
T	F	T
F	T	T
F	F	F

c.

p	q	$q \leftrightarrow \neg(p \wedge q)$
T	T	F
T	F	F
F	T	F
F	F	T

d.

p	q	$q \leftrightarrow \neg(p \wedge q)$
T	T	F
T	F	F
F	T	T
F	F	F

23. Which of the following characteristics accurately describes authentic assessment techniques?

a. They are norm-referenced
b. They are designed to build higher-order thinking skills
c. They allow students to choose from a set of teacher-prepared responses
d. They measure students' performance at a specific point in time

24. Given the partial table of values for $f(x)$ and $g(x)$, find $f(g(3))$. Assume that $f(x)$ and $g(x)$ are the simplest polynomials that fit the data.

x	$f(x)$	$g(x)$
−2	−16	−11
−1	−2	-8
0	0	-5
1	2	−2
2	16	1

a. 169
b. 128
c. 72
d. 16

25. Express the area of the given triangle as a function of x.

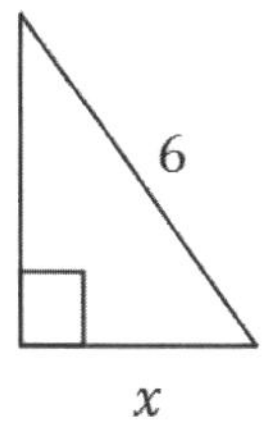

a. $A(x) = 3x$
b. $A(x) = \frac{x\sqrt{36-x^2}}{2}$
c. $A(x) = \frac{x^2}{2}$
d. $A(x) = 18 - \frac{x^2}{2}$

Refer to the following for question 26:

Below are graphed functions $f(x) = a_1 \sin(b_1 x)$ and $g(x) = a_2 \cos(b_2 x)$; a_1 and a_2 are integers, and b_1 and b_2 are positive rational numbers.

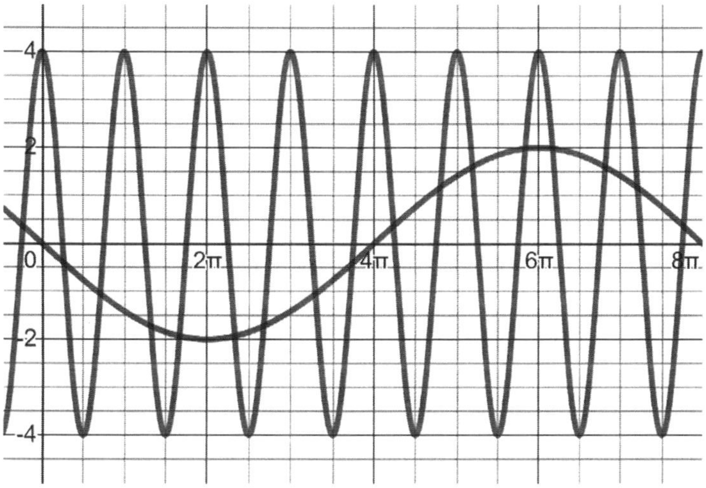

26. Which of the following statements is true?

a. $0 < a_2 < a_1$
b. $a_2 < 0 < a_1$
c. $0 < a_1 < a_2$
d. $a_1 < 0 < a_2$

27. Which of these correctly defines the recursive sequence $a_1 = -1, a_{n+1} = a_n + 2$ explicitly?

a. $a_n = 2n - 3$
b. $a_n = -n + 2$
c. $a_n = n - 2$
d. $a_n = -2n + 3$

28. Which mathematician is responsible for the formula for vertices, edges, and faces of a geometric solid: $V - E + F = 2$?

a. Pythagoras
b. Euclid
c. Euler
d. Fermat

29. Which of the following piecewise functions can describe the graph below?

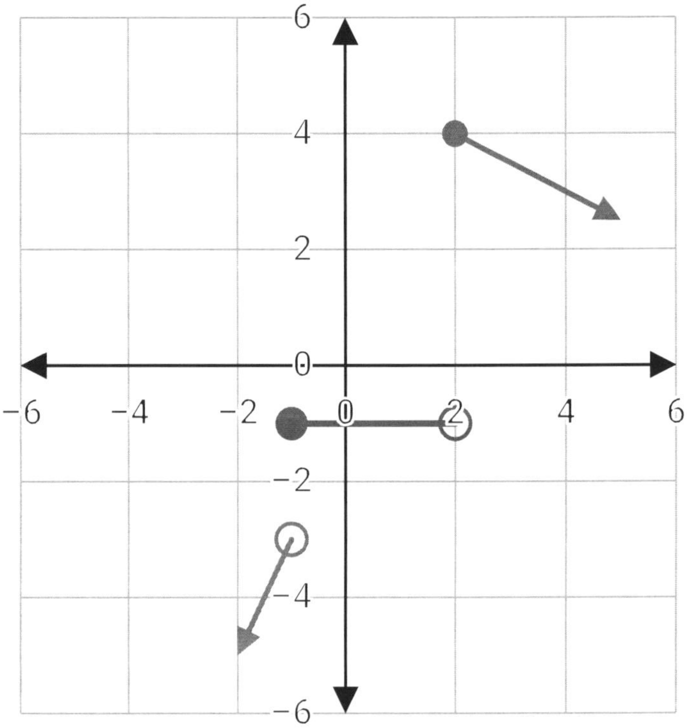

a. $f(x) = \begin{cases} 2x - 1 & x < -1 \\ -1 & -1 \le x < 2 \\ -\frac{1}{2}x + 5 & x \ge 2 \end{cases}$

b. $f(x) = \begin{cases} 2x - 1 & x \le -1 \\ [\![x]\!] & -1 \le x \le 2 \\ -x + 6 & x > 2 \end{cases}$

c. $f(x) = \begin{cases} 2x - 1 & x \le -1 \\ -1 & -1 < x \le 2 \\ -\frac{1}{2}x + 5 & x > 2 \end{cases}$

d. $f(x) = \begin{cases} x - 3 & x < -1 \\ -1 & -1 \le x < 2 \\ -2x + 5 & x \ge 2 \end{cases}$

Refer to the following for questions 30–31:

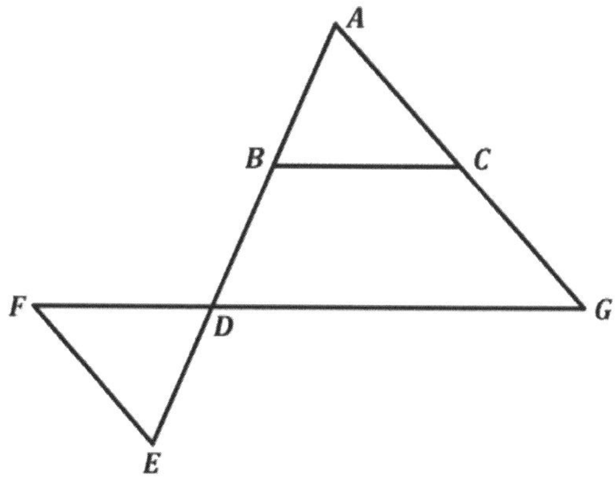

Statement	Reason
1. $\overline{BC} \parallel \overline{FG}$	Given
2.	
3. $\overline{FD} \cong \overline{BC}$	Given
4. $\overline{AB} \cong \overline{DE}$	Given
5. $\Delta ABC \cong \Delta EDF$	________
6. ________	
7. $\overline{FE} \parallel \overline{AG}$	

■

Given: $\overline{BC} \parallel \overline{FG}; \overline{FD} \cong \overline{BC}; \overline{AB} \cong \overline{DE}$

Prove: $\overline{FE} \parallel \overline{AG}$

30. Which of the following justifies step 5 in the proof?

a. AAS
b. SSS
c. ASA
d. SAS

31. Step 6 in the proof should contain which of the following statements?

a. $\angle BAC \cong \angle DEF$
b. $\angle ABC \cong \angle EDF$
c. $\angle ACB \cong \angle EFD$
d. $\angle GDA \cong \angle EDF$

32. The most effective way to structure a math session for the benefit of primary students is to:

a. Check all homework assignments and be sure that all workbook pages are completed
b. Focus almost entirely on computation skills
c. Focus almost entirely on the application of math skills to real-life situations
d. Divide class time evenly between computation skills and real-life applications

33. Which of these is a major contribution of the Greek civilization to the historical development of mathematics?

a. The division of an hour into 60 minutes, and a minute into 60 seconds, and a circle into 360 degrees
b. The development of algebra as a discipline separate from geometry
c. The use of deductive reasoning in geometric proofs
d. The introduction of Boolean logic

34. Which of the following expressions is equal to $\sin\theta\tan\theta$?

a. $\cot\theta$
b. $\tan\theta$
c. $\csc\theta - \sin\theta$
d. $\sec\theta - \cos\theta$

35. In the figure below, $ABCD$ is a parallelogram. The angles are $m\angle A = (5x)°$ and $m\angle B = (2x - 9)°$. Find $m\angle C$.

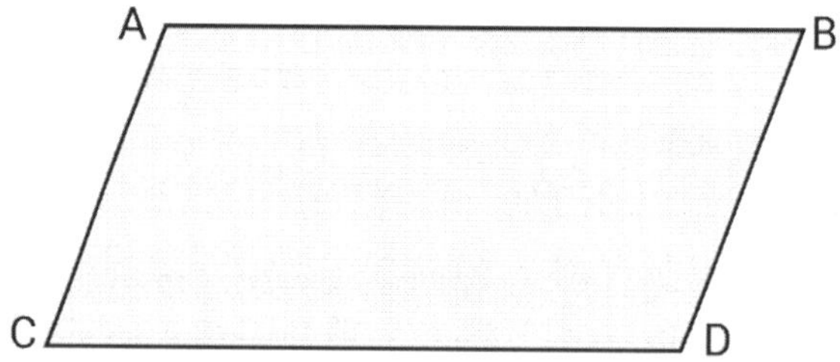

a. $m\angle C = 135°$
b. $m\angle C = 54°$
c. $m\angle C = 45°$
d. $m\angle C = 27°$

36. Mr. Reynold's students took a quiz on adding fractions. The work of one student is displayed below. Which choice best describes the student's work?

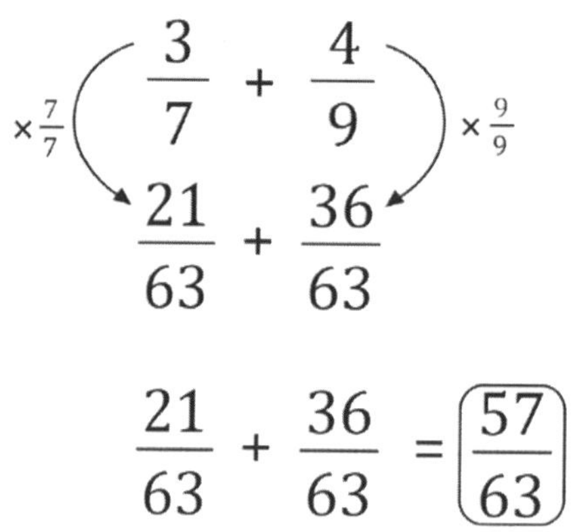

a. The student has calculated the correct answer. The sum of $\frac{3}{7}$ and $\frac{4}{9}$ is $\frac{57}{63}$.
b. The student has made an addition error in the last step. The sum of $\frac{21}{63}$ and $\frac{36}{63}$ is $\frac{67}{63}$, or $1\frac{4}{63}$.
c. The student has selected an incorrect common denominator. 63 is not the least common multiple for 7 and 9. The error resulted in an incorrect final answer.
d. The student has made an error in the multiplication process. 63 can be used as a common denominator, but the numerator in $\frac{3}{7}$ needs to be multiplied by 9, not 7. The numerator in $\frac{4}{9}$ needs to be multiplied by 7, not 9.

37. Which of the following is NOT a model that helps students understand subtraction?

a. Take away
b. Missing addend
c. Number line
d. Adding zero

38. The graph of $f(x)$ is a parabola with a focus of (a, b) and a directrix of $y = -b$, and $g(x)$ represents a transformation of $f(x)$. If the vertex of the graph of $g(x)$ is $(a, 0)$, which of these is a possible equation for $g(x)$ for nonzero integers a and b?

a. $g(x) = f(x) + b$
b. $g(x) = -f(x)$
c. $g(x) = f(x + a)$
d. $g(x) = f(x - a) + b$

39. Gene Y has three possible alleles, or gene forms, called a, b and c. Each individual carries two copies of Gene Y, one of which is inherited from his or her mother and the other of which is inherited from his or her father. If the two copies of Gene Y are of the same form, the individual is homozygous for that allele; otherwise, the individual is heterozygous. The following table represents genetic data from 1,000 individuals selected at random from the population.

		Allele 2		
		a	b	c
Allele 1	a	136	72	29
	b	132	213	141
	c	32	65	180

Using experimental probability, predict the number of individuals in a population of 10,000 who will be homozygous for any allele.

a. 4,710
b. 4,920
c. 5,080
d. 5,290

40. Which of these would best illustrate change over time?

a. Pie chart
b. Line graph
c. Box-and-whisker plot
d. Venn diagram

Refer to the following for question 41:

The box-and-whisker plot displays student test scores assessed throughout a semester to see if students were improving.

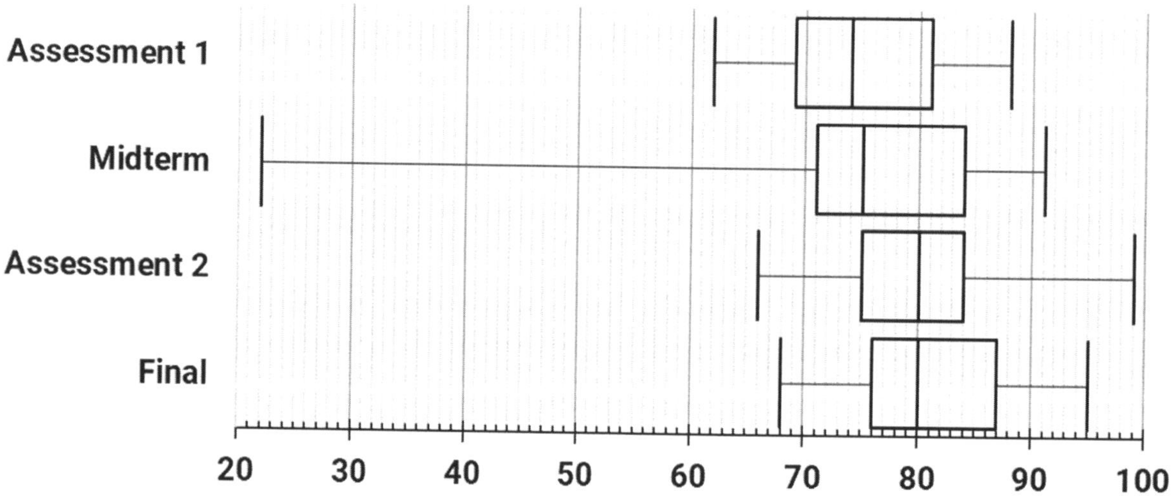

41. What is the probability that a test score chosen at random from the Final is less than 87?

a. 0.25
b. 0.5
c. 0.6
d. 0.75

42. A water tower is in the shape of a cylinder with a diameter of 840 in and a height of 220 in. How much water can it hold when completely full?

a. $5.54x10^5$ in^3
b. $1.69x10^6$ in^3
c. $1.22x10^8$ in^3
d. $4.87x10^8$ in^3

43. A student is asked to find 3/5 of 75. Which of the following expressions could the student use?

a. $(3 \times 75) \div 5$
b. $75 \div 0.6$
c. Either A or B
d. Neither A nor B

44. In how many distinguishable ways can a family of five be seated at a circular table with five chairs if Tasha and Mac must be kept separated by at least one chair?

a. 6
b. 12
c. 24
d. 60

45. Mr. Omari's students are learning how to use a variety of tools and models to help them convert between equivalent decimals, fractions, and percents. He gives them the following problem:

Put the following in order from smallest to greatest: 0.75, $\frac{3}{5}$, 80%

Which of the following tools best corresponds to this task?

a. Pieces of play clay
b. Money
c. Drawing a visual representation
d. Interlocking cubes

46. To test the accuracy and precision of two scales, a student repeatedly measured the mass of a 5g standard and recorded these results.

	Trial 1	Trial 2	Trial 3	Trial 4
Scale 1	4.98 g	4.97 g	4.99 g	5.03 g
Scale 2	5.01 g	4.99 g	5.02 g	5.01 g

Which of these conclusions about the scales is true?

a. Scale 1 has an average percent error of 0.45%, and Scale 2 has an average percent error of 0.25%. Scale 2 is more accurate and precise than Scale 1.
b. Scale 1 has an average percent error of 0.45%, and Scale 2 has an average percent error of 0.25%. Scale 2 is more accurate than Scale 1; however, Scale 1 is more precise.
c. Scale 1 has an average percent error of 0.2%, and Scale 2 has an average percent error of 0.4%. Scale 1 is more accurate and precise than Scale 2.
d. Scale 1 has an average percent error of 0.2%, and Scale 2 has an average percent error of 0.4%. Scale 1 is more accurate than Scale 2; however, Scale 2 is more precise.

47. Which of these statements is (are) true for the function $g(x)$?

$$g(x) = \begin{cases} x & x < 2 \\ -\frac{1}{2}x + 3 & x \geq 2 \end{cases}$$

I. $g(1) = 1$
II. The domain of $g(x)$ is all real numbers.
III. The range of $g(x)$ is $y \geq 2$.

a. II only
b. III only
c. I and II
d. I, II, and III

48. If the diameter of Circle A is 12 cm and the radius of circle B is 15 cm, what is the ratio of the area of Circle A to the area of Circle B?

a. $\frac{4}{25}$
b. $\frac{16}{25}$
c. $\frac{2}{5}$
d. $\frac{4}{5}$

49. Which of these is the equation of the function graphed below?

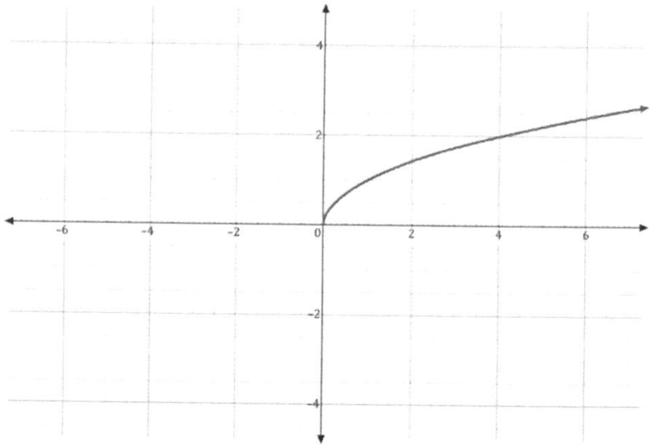

a. $f(x) = x^2$
b. $f(x) = \sqrt{x}$
c. $f(x) = 2^x$
d. $f(x) = \log_2 x$

50. What is the converse of the statement below?

If I go skiing, then it is winter.

a. If it is not winter, then I do not go skiing.
b. If it is winter, then I go skiing.
c. If it is not winter, then I go skiing.
d. If I go skiing, then it is not winter.

51. Which of these can be modeled by an exponential function?

a. The path of a sound wave
b. The path of a ball being kicked into the air
c. The distance an object travels over time when the rate is constant
d. Radioactive decay

52. Two teachers from a county are chosen at random to attend a conference for high school science educators. What is the approximate probability that two women from the same department will be chosen?

	Biology	Chemistry	Physics
Women	26	31	20
Men	16	11	25

a. 8.6%
b. 10.7%
c. 11.9%
d. 13.8%

53. Complete the analogy: $y = \frac{1}{\sqrt{x}}$ is to $x = y^{-2}$ as ...

a. $y = 2x$ is to $x = y^2$.
b. $y = e^x$ is to $x = \frac{1}{e^y}$, where $y > 0$.
c. $y = \frac{1}{x^2}$ is to $x = y^2$, where $x, y \neq 0$.
d. $y = \cos x$ is to $x = \cos^{-1} y$.

54. If a, b, and c are multiples of 6 and $3a^2 + 2b^3 = c$, of the following integers, which is the largest integer that must be factor of c?

a. 6
b. 36
c. 72
d. 108

55. Levi walked to the grocery store and back. The graph below shows his distance from home at times throughout the walk. If the y-axis represents the distance from home in miles and the x-axis represents the number of hours he was gone, which of the following statements is (are) true?

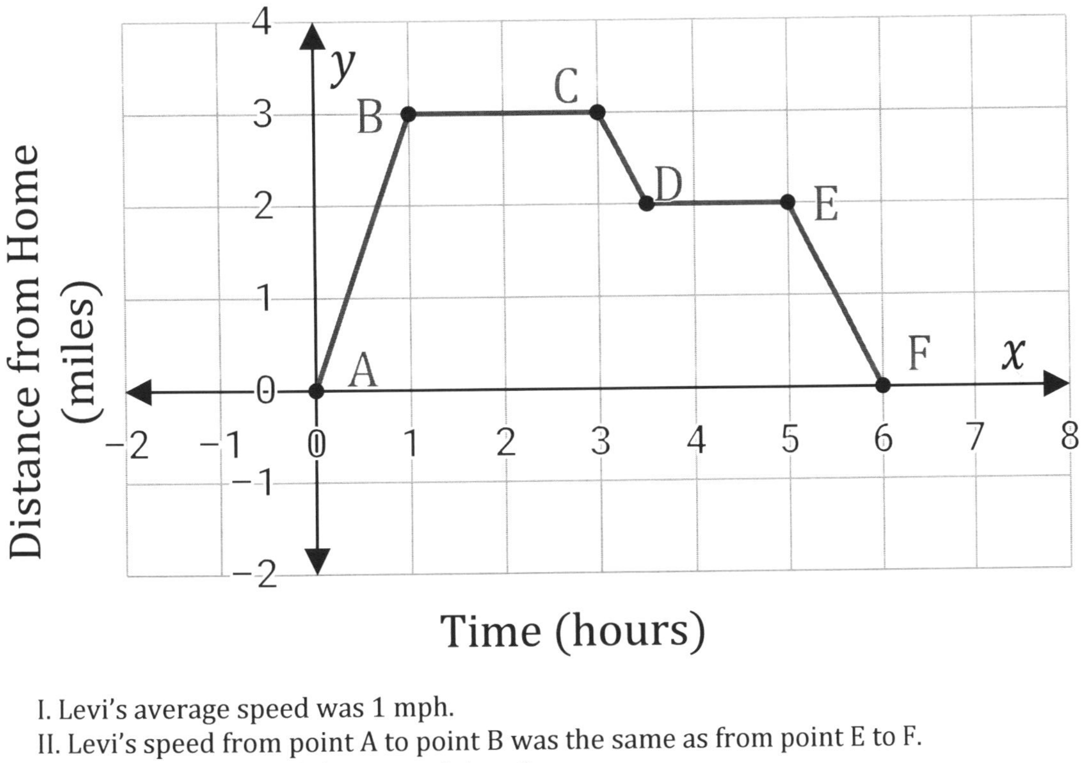

I. Levi's average speed was 1 mph.
II. Levi's speed from point A to point B was the same as from point E to F.
III. Levi walked a total distance of six miles.

a. I only
b. II only
c. I and II
d. I and III

56. A pasta salad was chilled in the refrigerator at 35° F overnight for 9 hours. The temperature of the pasta dish dropped from 86° F to 38° F. What was the average rate of cooling per hour?

a. 4.8°/hr
b. 5.3°/hr
c. 5.15°/hr
d. 0.532°/hr

57. Ben is purchasing notebooks and boxes of pencils for a class he is teaching. Notebooks cost \$1 each and pencils cost \$3 per box. If the x-axis represents boxes of pencils, the y-axis represents notebooks, and Ben can spend a maximum of \$30, which of the following graphs shows the number of notebooks and pencils Ben can purchase?

a. 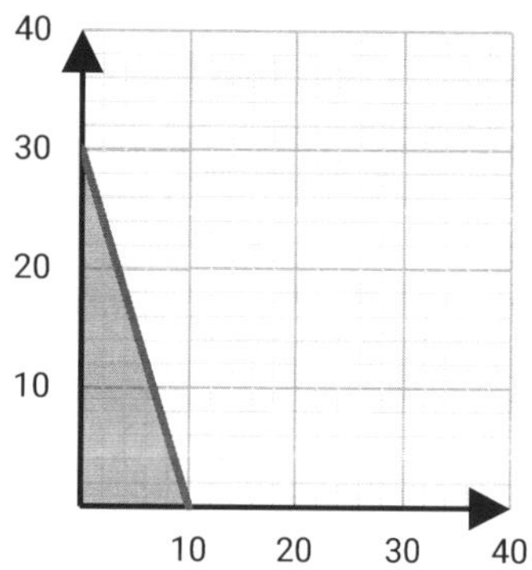

c. 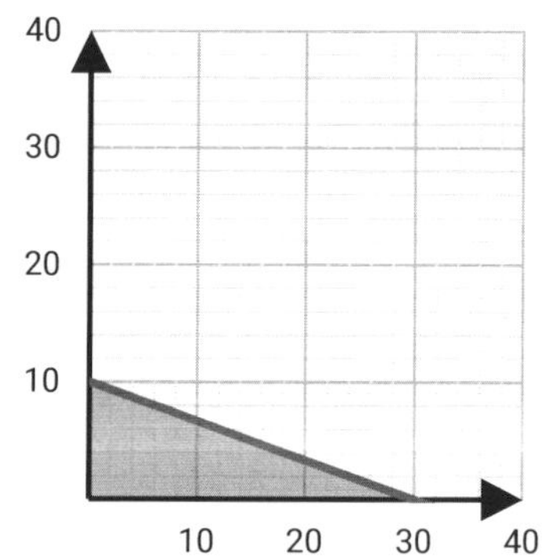

b. 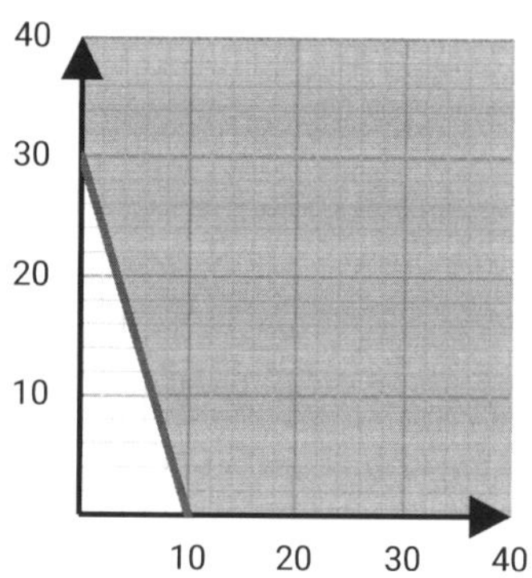

d. 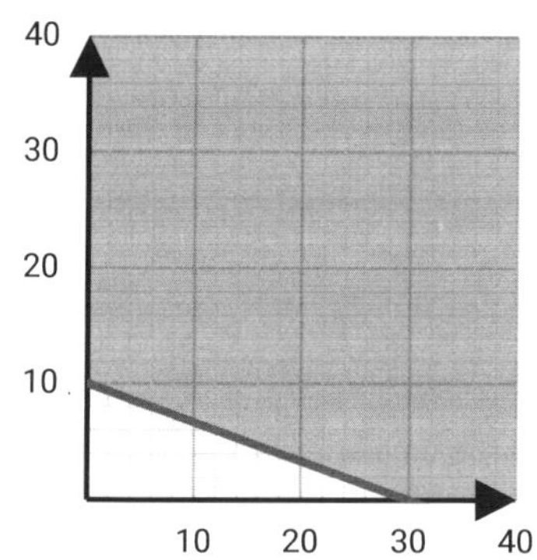

58. A triangle has side lengths of 19.7 cm, 20.4 cm, and 10.2 cm. Round each length to the nearest ten centimeters and estimate the perimeter of the triangle.

a. 60 cm
b. 50 cm
c. 55 cm
d. 65 cm

59. The high school honors program is offering three special electives: Biophysics, Intro to Law, and Latin. Seventeen students enrolled in Biophysics, twenty-two in Intro to Law, and nineteen in Latin. Two students are taking both Biophysics and Intro to Law, seven are taking both Intro to Law and Latin, and four are taking both Biophysics and Latin. One student enrolled in all three electives. How many students are taking special electives?

a. 46
b. 49
c. 55
d. 58

60. Which number should fill in the blank in the sequence 18, 23, 27, __, 32, 33?

a. 28
b. 29
c. 30
d. 31

61. Two companies offer monthly cell phone plans, both of which include free text messaging. Company A charges a \$25 monthly fee plus five cents per minute of phone conversation, while Company B charges a \$50 monthly fee and offers unlimited calling. At what total duration of monthly calls do both companies charge the same amount?

a. 500 hours
b. 8 hours and 33 minutes
c. 8 hours and 20 minutes
d. 5 hours

62. Which of the following statements is (are) true when $f(x) = \frac{x^2-x-2}{x^3-7x+6}$?

I. The graph $f(x)$ has vertical asymptotes at $x = -3$, $x = 1$, and $x = 2$.
II. The x- and y-intercepts of the graph of $f(x)$ are both $-\frac{1}{3}$.

a. I only
b. II only
c. I and II
d. Neither statement is true.

63. Which of these defines the recursive sequence $a_1 = 2$, $a_{n+1} = a_n - 3$ explicitly?

a. $a_n = 2n - 3$
b. $a_n = -3n + 5$
c. $a_n = n - 1$
d. $a_n = -2n + 2$

64. Solve the system of equations: $\begin{cases} 3x + y = 1 \\ -4x + 3y = 29 \end{cases}$.

a. $(-2, 7)$
b. $(-1, 3)$
c. $\left(0, \frac{1}{2}\right)$
d. $\left(2, -\frac{5}{2}\right)$

65. If $f(x) = 4x^3 - x^2 - 4x + 2$, which of the following statements is (are) true of its graph?

I. The point $\left(-\frac{1}{2}, 3\frac{1}{4}\right)$ is a relative maximum.

II. The graph of f is concave upward on the interval $(-\infty, \frac{1}{12})$.

a. I
b. II
c. I and II
d. Neither I nor II

66. The test scores of 250 students are normally distributed with a mean score of 84 and a standard deviation of 7. In a normal distribution, approximately 68% of values are within one standard deviation of the mean. About how many students scored 91 or higher?

a. 16
b. 40
c. 88
d. 102

67. Kayla has a $75 budget to purchase gifts for her colleagues. She wants to buy coffee mugs and note pads. She may purchase a maximum of 30 items. Each coffee mug costs $6 and each note pad costs $3. Which of the following graphs correctly shows the possible combinations of coffee mugs and note pads that she may buy?

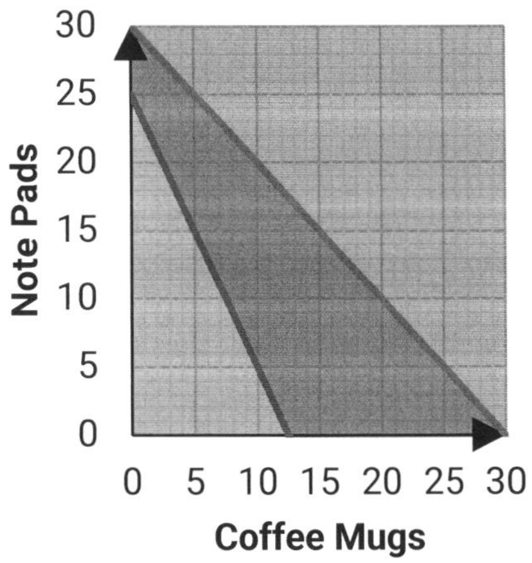

a.

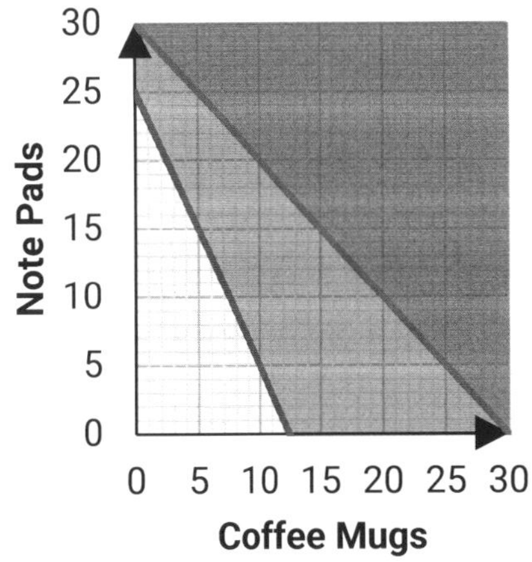

b.

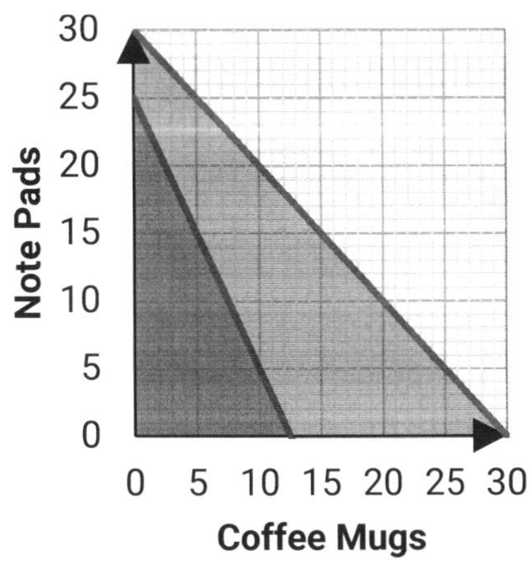

c.

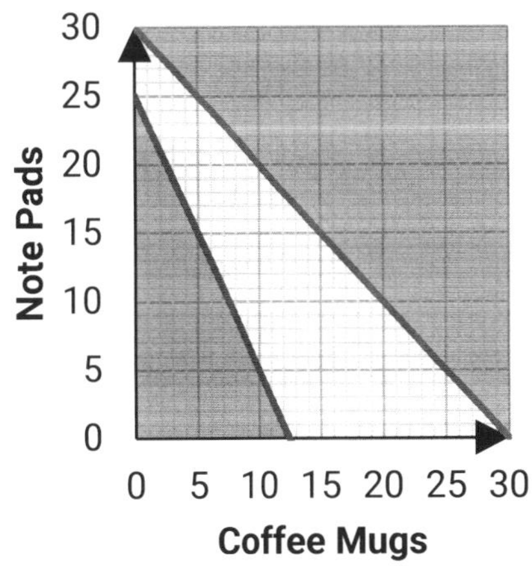

d.

68. At today's visit to her doctor, Josephine was prescribed a liquid medication with instructions to take 25 cc's every four hours. She filled the prescription on her way to work, but when it came time to take the medicine, she realized that the pharmacist did not include a measuring cup. Josephine estimated that the plastic spoon in her desk drawer was about the same size as a teaspoon and decided to use it to measure the approximate dosage. She recalled that one cubic centimeter (cc) is equal to one milliliter (mL) but was not sure how many milliliters were in a teaspoon. So, she noted that a two-liter bottle of soda contains about the same amount as a half-gallon container of milk and applied her knowledge of the customary system of measurement to determine how many teaspoons of medicine to take. Which of these calculations might she have used to approximate her dosage?

a. $25 \times \frac{1}{1{,}000} \times \frac{2}{0.5} \times 16 \times 48$
b. $25 \times \frac{1}{100} \times \frac{0.5}{2} \times 16 \times 4 \times 12$
c. $\frac{1{,}000}{25} \times \frac{0.5}{2} \times 16 \times 4 \times 12$
d. $\frac{25}{1{,}000} \times \frac{1}{4} \times 16 \times 48$

69. Simplify:

$$\frac{(x^2y^{-3})(4xy)^2}{16x^4y^4} + \frac{3}{2xy}$$

a. $\frac{3x+24y^6}{8xy^7}$
b. $\frac{2x+6y^6}{2xy^4}$
c. $\frac{x+24y^5}{8xy^6}$
d. $\frac{2x+3y^4}{2xy^5}$

70. If $f(x) = \tan(2x + 4)$, then $f^{-1}(x) =$

a. $\frac{1}{2}\tan^{-1}(x) - 2$
b. $\sec(2x + 4)$
c. $\tan^{-1}\left(\frac{1}{2}x - 2\right)$
d. $2\tan^{-1}(x) - 4$

71. What number should come next in the sequence: 3, 6, 8, 16, 18, 36, ...?

a. 38
b. 44
c. 57
d. 72

72. Solve the system of equations.

$$\begin{cases} 2x - 4y + z = 10 \\ -3x + 2y - 4z = -7 \\ x + y - 3z = -1 \end{cases}$$

a. $(-1, -3, 0)$
b. $(-\frac{3}{4}, -\frac{21}{8}, -1)$
c. $(1, -2, 0)$
d. No solution

73. Which of these would best illustrate the distribution of data across a range?

a. Pie chart
b. Line graph
c. Box-and-whisker plot
d. Venn diagram

74. Which of the following expressions is equivalent to $\sin 2x \sec x$?

a. 1
b. $2 \sin x$
c. $2 \cos x$
d. $\tan 2x$

75. The vertices of a polygon are $(0, 3)$, $(1, -1)$, $(3, 3)$, and $(4, -1)$. Which of the following describes the polygon most specifically?

a. Parallelogram
b. Rhombus
c. Rectangle
d. Square

76. A dress is marked down by 20% and placed on a clearance rack, under a sign reading "Take an extra 25% off already reduced merchandise." What fraction of the original price is the final sale price of the dress?

a. $\frac{2}{5}$
b. $\frac{9}{20}$
c. $\frac{3}{5}$
d. $\frac{11}{20}$

Refer to the following for question 77:

The box-and-whisker plot displays student test scores assessed throughout a semester to see if students were improving.

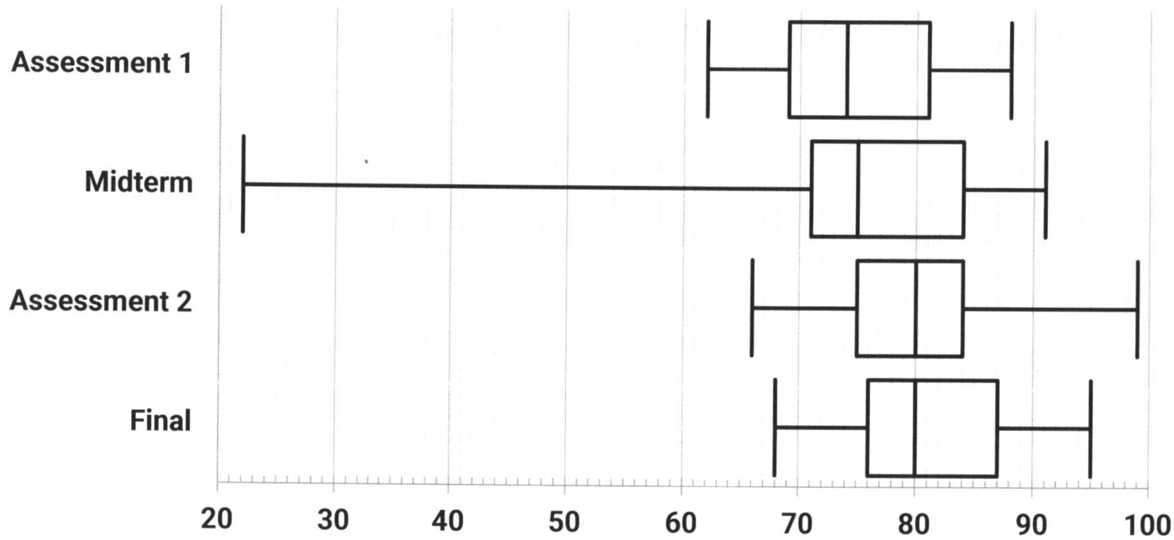

77. Which of the following statements is necessarily true of the data?

a. The mean better reflects student performance at the midterm than the median.
b. The mean test score for assessment 2 and the final is the same.
c. Assessment 1 had the highest median grade.
d. The median test score is below the mean for assessment 2.

78. Find $(g \circ f)(x)$ when $f(x) = 3x - 2$ and $g(x) = x^2 - x - 6$.

a. $9x^2 - 6x + 6$
b. $3x^2 - 9x + 8$
c. $9x^2 - 15x$
d. $3x^2 - 12x + 2$

79. In the triangle, which of the following is equal to $\sin\theta$?

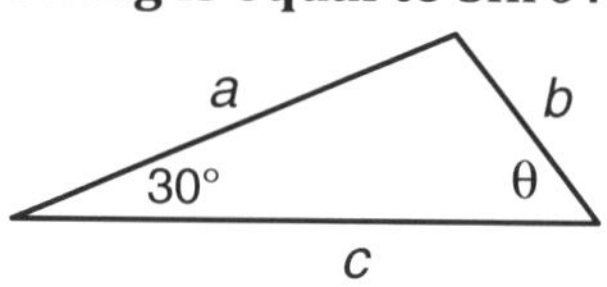

a. $\frac{a}{2b}$
b. $\frac{2b}{a}$
c. $\frac{a}{2c}$
d. $\frac{b}{ac}$

80. Which of these statements is NOT necessarily true when $f(x) = \log_b x$ and $b > 1$?

a. The x-intercept of the graph of $f(x)$ is 1.
b. The graph of $f(x)$ passes through $(b, 1)$.

c. $f(x)$ is undefined when $x < 1$.
d. If $g(x) = b^x$, the graph of $f(x)$ is symmetric to the graph of $g(x)$ with respect to $y = x$.

81. A cube inscribed in a sphere has a volume of 64 cubic units. What is the volume of the sphere in cubic units?

a. $4\pi\sqrt{3}$
b. $8\pi\sqrt{3}$
c. $32\pi\sqrt{3}$
d. $256\pi\sqrt{3}$

82. Identify a possible cross-section polygon NOT formed by a plane containing the given points on the cube.

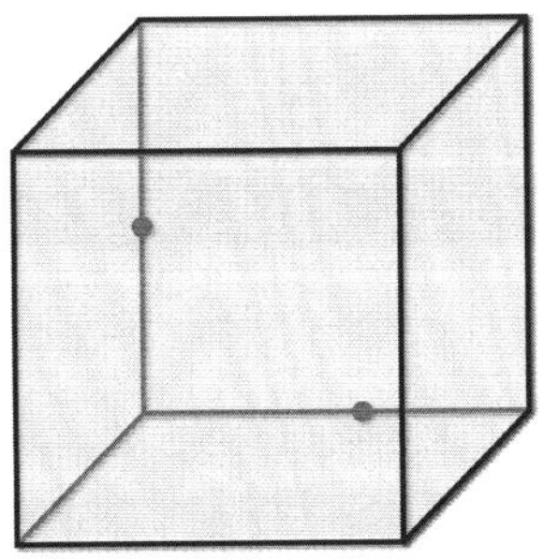

a. Triangle
b. Square
c. Pentagon
d. Hexagon

83. Solve $x^4 + 225 = 34x^2$.

a. $x = \{3, 5\}$
b. $x = \{3i, 5i\}$
c. $x = \{-5, -3, 3, 5\}$
d. $x = \{-5i, -3i, 3i, 5i\}$

Refer to the following for question 84:

For a science fair project, Paul wanted to find the probability of rolling an even number with a weighted die versus a fair die. He did fifty tests, rolling the die three times for each test and recording the number of even numbers that came up. The chart below shows his results.

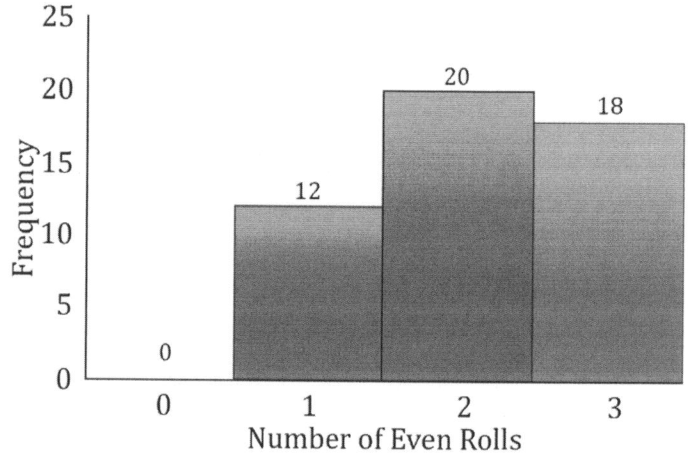

84. Which of these shows the graphs of the probability distributions (probability of rolling an even) from five rolls of this unevenly-weighted die and five rolls of a fair die?

a. 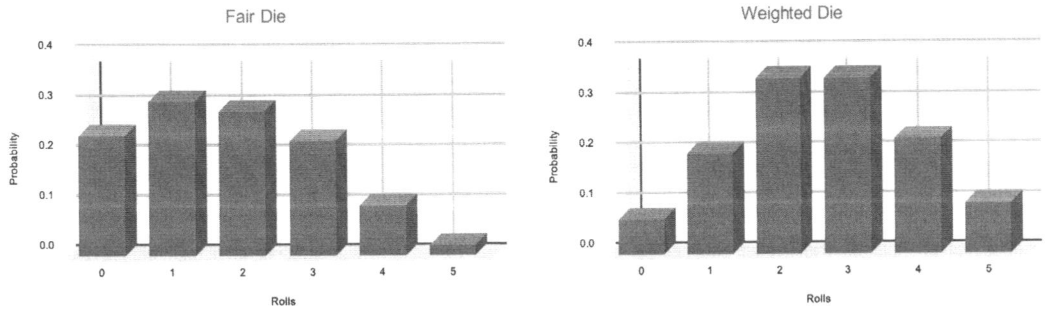

b. 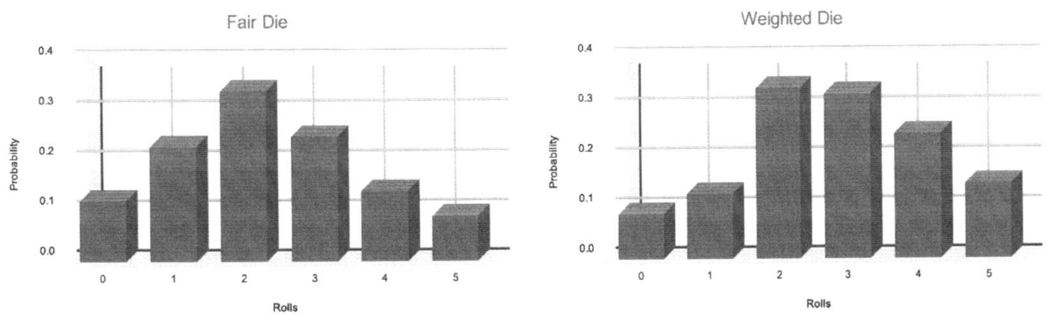

c. 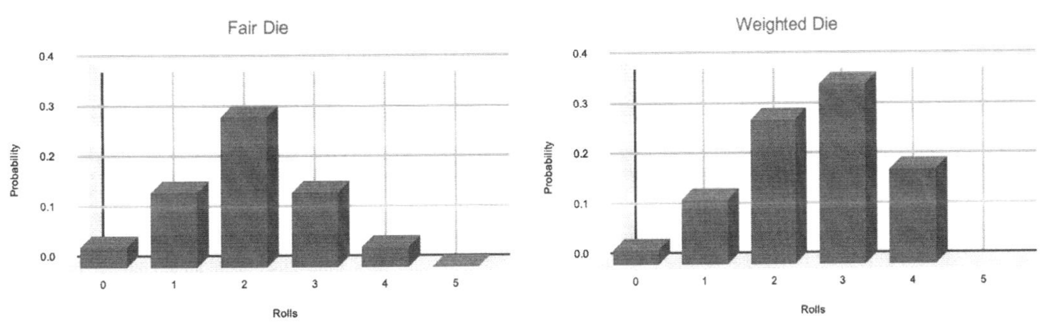

d. None of the above

85. What is a disadvantage of using rubrics as assessment tools?

a. Learning objectives, tasks, guidance, and criteria are combined.
b. Performance levels are not as precise as grades or percentages.
c. They afford greater brevity in definition, guidance, assessment.
d. Rubrics are more concise yet offer more clarity than other tools.

86. For vector $v = (4, 3)$ and vector $w = (-3, 4)$, find $2(v + w)$.

a. $(2, 14)$
b. $(14, -2)$
c. $(1,7)$
d. $(7, -1)$

87. Which of these is NOT a net of a rectangular prism?

a. 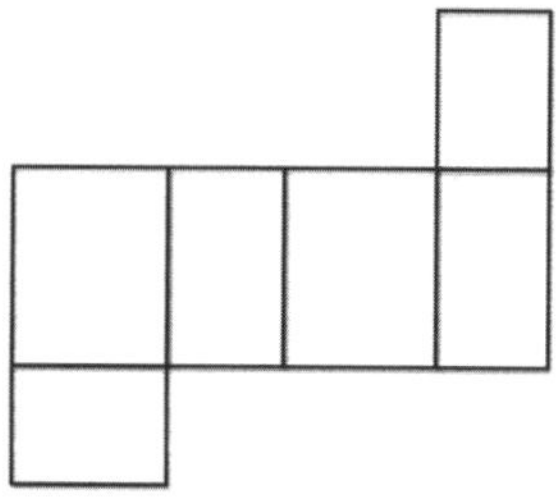

b. 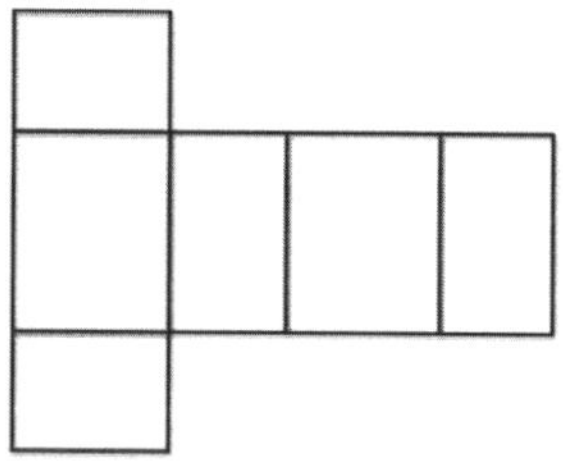

c. 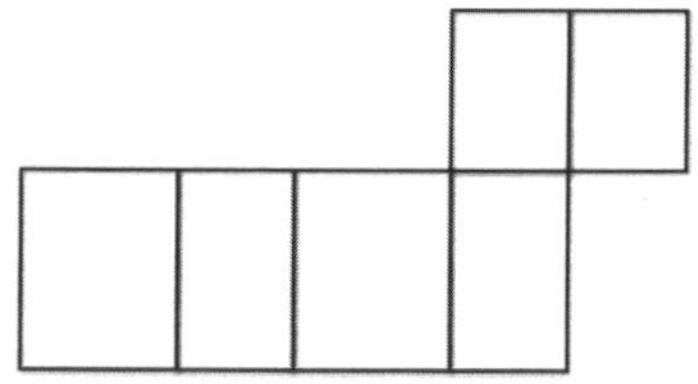

d. 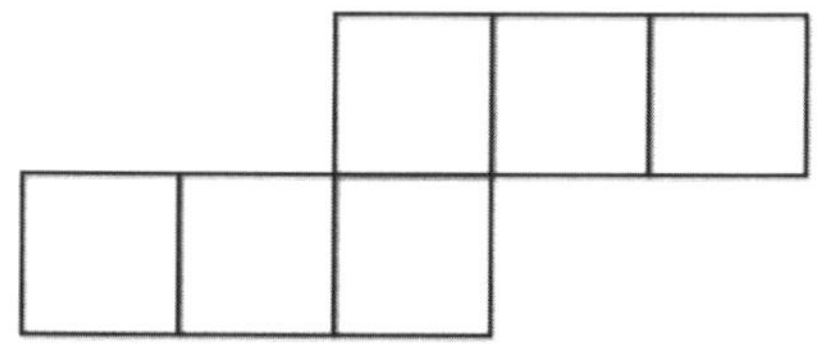

Refer to the following for questions 88–89:

The box-and-whisker plot displays a district's standardized test scores by subject.

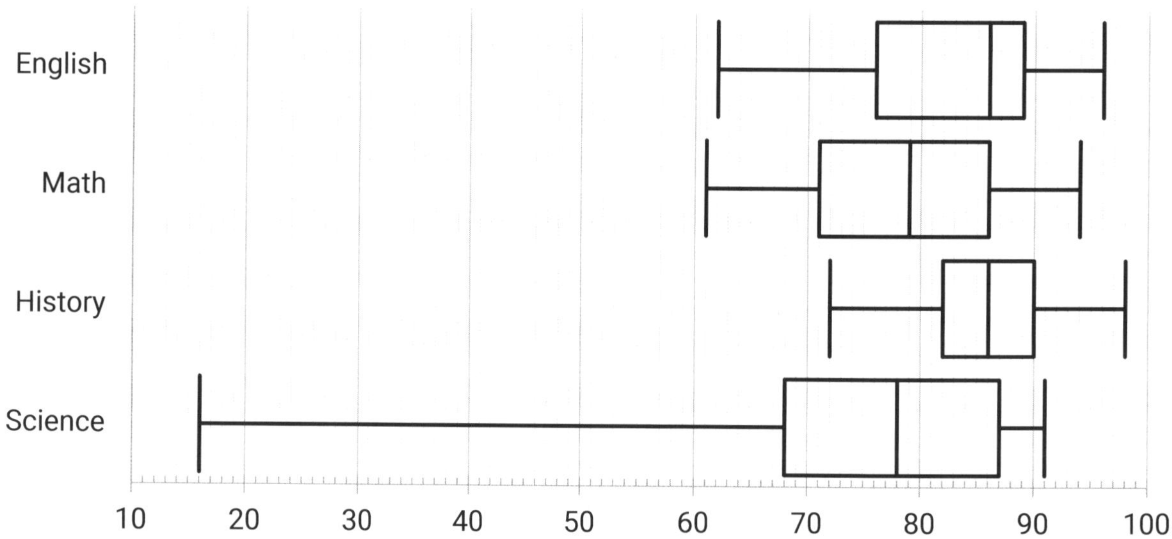

88. What is the probability that a student chosen at random from Math made above an 86 on this test?

a. 25%
b. 50%
c. 60%
d. 75%

89. Which of the following statements is NOT true of the data?

a. The median better reflects student performance in Science than the mean.
b. The mean test score for English and history is the same.
c. The median of the History scores is the same as the 3rd quartile score for Math.
d. The median test score is above the mean for English.

90. If $\sin\theta = \frac{\sqrt{2}}{2}$ when $\frac{\pi}{2} < \theta < \pi$, what is the value of θ?

a. $\frac{\pi}{4}$
b. $\frac{3\pi}{4}$
c. $\frac{2\pi}{3}$
d. $\frac{5\pi}{6}$

91. Identify the cross-section polygon formed by a plane containing the given points on the cube.

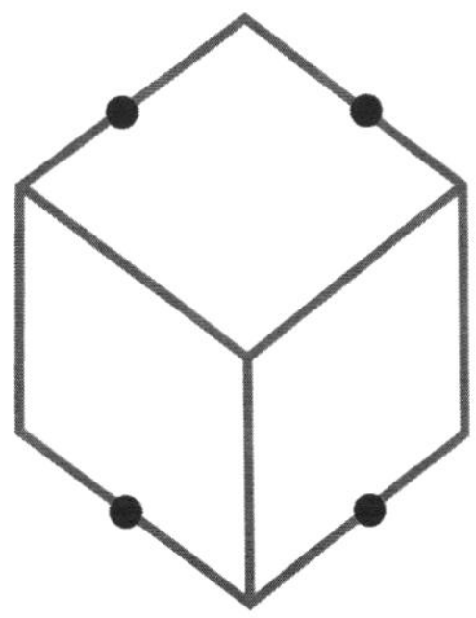

a. Rectangle
b. Trapezoid
c. Pentagon
d. Hexagon

92. If the midpoint of a line segment graphed on the xy-coordinate plane is $(-2, 3)$ and the slope of the line segment is $-\frac{1}{2}$, which of these is a possible endpoint of the line segment?

a. $(-4,3)$
b. $(2,1)$
c. $(-6,6)$
d. $\left(0,\frac{3}{2}\right)$

93. Mrs. Wilson is working with a group of 5th graders. She asks her students to solve the multiplication problem $\frac{1}{3} \times \frac{1}{4}$ using a model. The work of one of her students is illustrated below.

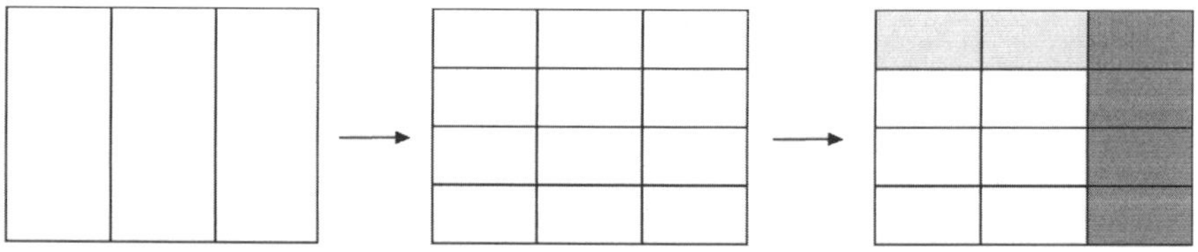

The student claims that the correct answer is $\frac{6}{12}$ because 6 total pieces are shaded. How would you describe the student's error?

a. The student's error is that they drew a model for $\frac{1}{3} \div \frac{1}{4}$ instead of $\frac{1}{3} \times \frac{1}{4}$.

b. The student has correctly shaded $\frac{1}{3}$ and $\frac{1}{4}$ of the model. However, the student has misidentified the answer within the model. The answer is not the total number of shaded pieces, but the total number of overlapping pieces, which in this case is 1. The answer should be $\frac{1}{12}$.

c. The student's error is that the models cannot be drawn using rectangles, they must be drawn using circles.

d. The student has correctly shaded $\frac{1}{3}$ and $\frac{1}{4}$ of the model. However, the student has misidentified the answer within the model. The answer is determined by subtracting the vertical "parts" by the horizontal "parts." In this case, $4 - 3$. The answer is 1.

94. Which of the graphs shown represents $f(x) = 2|-x - 1| + 2$?

a.

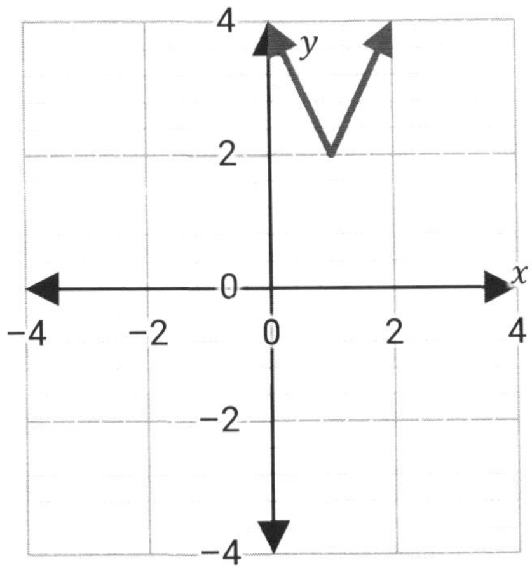

c.

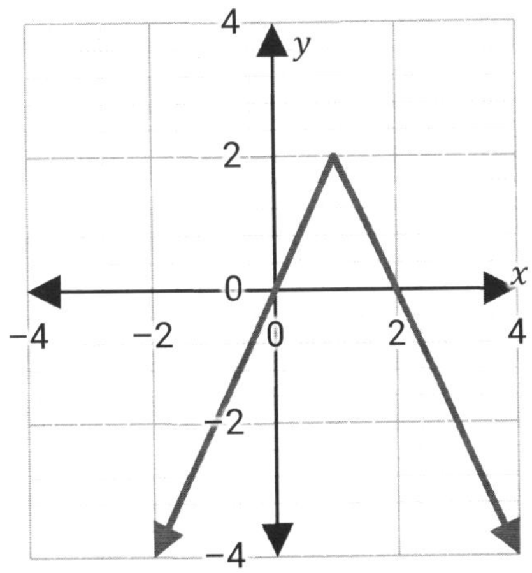

b.

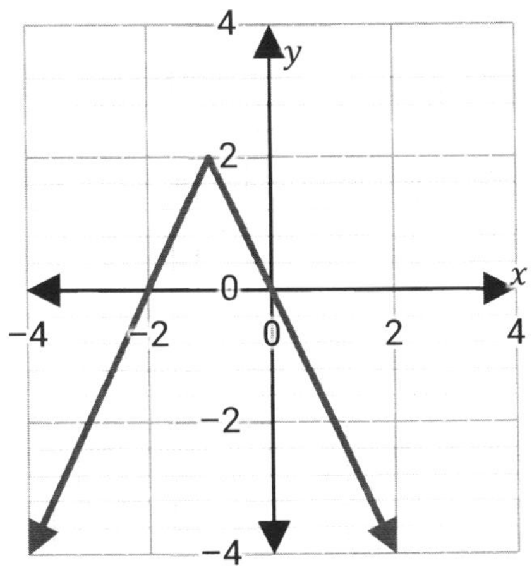

d.

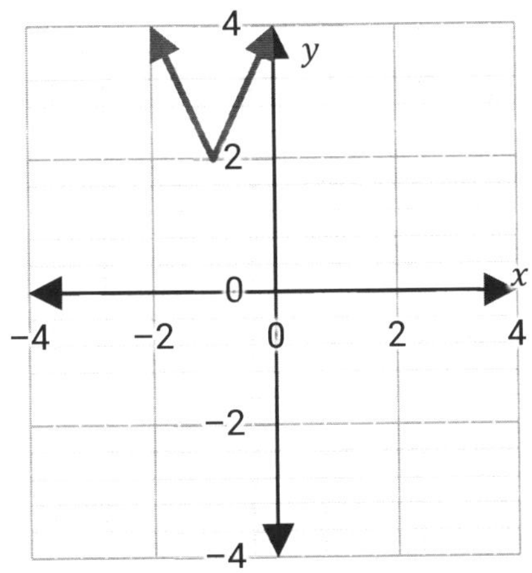

95. A small company is divided into three departments, as shown. Two individuals are chosen at random to attend a conference. What is the approximate probability that two women from the same department will be chosen?

	Department 1	Department 2	Department 3
Women	12	28	16
Men	18	14	15

a. 8.6%
b. 10.7%
c. 11.2%
d. 13.8%

96. Marcus is putting chicken wire around his rectangular garden. He decides to add cantaloupes to his garden, so he needs to expand the size of the garden. He finds that by moving the boundary line back x feet on each of the four sides, he fences a rectangular space 34 yd^2 larger than the original plan and spends an extra $36 on fencing, which costs $1.50 per linear foot. How much does he spend?

a. $145.50
b. $171
c. $223.50
d. $352

97. Keisha is solving a problem asking her to mix lemonade from a powder mix:

> The instructions on the lemonade label say "To make 8 cups of lemonade, mix 1 cup powder with 8 cups of water". You need 24 cups of lemonade. How much powder should you use?

Keisha writes that she will need 17 cups of lemonade powder. Which teacher prompt best addresses Keisha's error and helps her find the correct answer?

a. "It looks like you multiplied 8 by 2 instead of 3. Let's try multiplying by 3."
b. "It looks like you added 16 cups to both the lemonade powder and the water. Could you instead tell me how many batches of 8 cups you will need to make in order to get 24 cups?"
c. Both (a) and (b)
d. Neither (a) nor (b)

98. Chan receives a bonus from his job. He pays 30% in taxes, gives 30% to charity, and uses another 25% to pay off an old debt. He has $600 left. What was the total amount of Chan's bonus?

a. $4,000
b. $3,600
c. $3,200
d. $3,000

99. For which of these does a rotation of 120° about the center of the polygon map the polygon onto itself?

a. Square
b. Regular hexagon
c. Regular octagon
d. Regular decagon

100. If a, b, and c are multiples of 3 and $4a^2 + b^3 = c$, which of these is the largest number that must be factor of c?

a. 3
b. 6
c. 9
d. 12

Answer Key and Explanations for Test #1

1. D: Let b represent the base of the triangle. The height h of the triangle is the altitude drawn from the vertex opposite of b to side b.

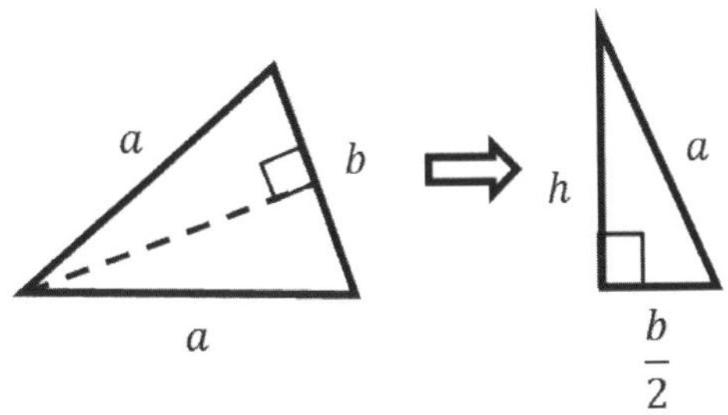

The height of the triangle can be found in terms of a and b by using the Pythagorean theorem.

$$h^2 + \left(\frac{b}{2}\right)^2 = a^2$$

$$h = \sqrt{a^2 - \frac{b^2}{4}}$$

$$h = \sqrt{\frac{4a^2 - b^2}{4}}$$

$$h = \frac{\sqrt{4a^2 - b^2}}{2}$$

The area of a triangle is $A = \frac{1}{2}bh$, so $A = \frac{1}{2}b\left(\frac{\sqrt{4a^2-b^2}}{2}\right) = \frac{b\sqrt{4a^2-b^2}}{4}$.

2. C: When rolling two dice, there is only one way to roll a sum of 2 (rolling a 1 on each die) and 12 (rolling 6 on each die). In contrast, there are two ways to obtain a sum of 3 (rolling a 2 and 1 or a 1 and 2) and 11 (rolling a 5 and 6 or a 6 and 5), three ways to obtain a sum of 4 (1 and 3; 2 and 2; 3 and 1) or 10 (4 and 6; 5 and 5; 6 and 4), and so on. Since the probability of obtaining each sum is inconsistent, this is not a random selection.

3. C: A quick estimation of the number of feet the mountain climber climbs is found by rounding each day's climb to the nearest hundred feet and finding the sum. 480 rounds to 500, 610 rounds to 600, 295 rounds to 300, and 303 also rounds to 300.

$$500 + 600 + 300 + 300 = 1{,}700$$

Therefore, she climbed approximately 1,700 feet.

4. D: In choice A, the teacher uses convenience sampling, which is a biased technique. A group of athletes is likely not representative of all high school girls. Choice B also represents convenience sampling, as all surveys were taken from the same neighborhood. While this likely included a variety of ages, career paths, etc., it most likely represented a narrow demographic since homes in a neighborhood tend to be similar in value. Choice C is biased because the participants are self-selected rather than randomly selected. It may be that people who have a strong opinion are more likely to respond than those who are more neutral, and this would give a skewed perspective of opinions. Choice D represents random selection since names are organized by computer generation rather than any particular demographic.

5. A: The teacher is looking to teach about perimeter and area, a skill which applies only to two-dimensional shapes. The activity the teacher wants to use focuses on "using appropriate tools strategically," which means that the students should have an assortment of tools to use.

A good activity for teaching those skills is to provide students with shapes to find the area of. Shapes can include straight-edged shapes like squares and triangles, but they can also include circles or other shapes with rounded edges. The activity that is chosen needs to accommodate a variety of shapes, which is why the students would need yarn to trace curved edges and a ruler to measure the yarn or straight edges. The teacher should also be interested in having all students do the same activity to help make grading fair and possible, so using worksheets is probably a good idea but not the only option.

Choices B, C, and D all refer to "objects," which are three-dimensional. Surface area and volume are skills that build on area and perimeter, so a teacher would want to be careful about selecting a task that can be easily followed by the students. Choice B focuses on calculation and not on using appropriate tools. Choice C provides only one tool for the job, and may not accommodate curved shapes. Choice D also only provides the students with one tool to use, and it is a tool that is not typically used in the real world. Choice A is the best option because it requires the students to think strategically about what tools to use to obtain a measurement and calculate both perimeter and area. Keep in mind that an activity does not need to target all objectives at once, so it is okay if the teacher decided to have the students calculate only perimeter or only area.

6. C: If $y = a(x+b)^2(x+c)^2$, the degree of the polynomial is 4. Since the degree of the polynomial is even and the leading coefficient is positive ($a > 0$), the end behavior of the graph goes to (∞, ∞) and $(-\infty, \infty)$. Therefore, only Choice C is a possible graph of this function.

7. C: When the shirt is marked down by 25%, the cost of the shirt is 75% of its original price. Therefore, the reduced price of the shirt can be written as $\frac{75}{100}x$, or $\frac{3}{4}x$, where x is the original price. When discounted an extra 30%, the shirt costs 70% of the reduced price, or $\frac{70}{100}\left(\frac{3}{4}x\right)$, or $\frac{7}{10}\left(\frac{3}{4}x\right)$, which simplifies to $\frac{21}{40}x$. So, the final price is $\frac{21}{40}$ of the original price.

8. C: On the unit circle, $\sin\theta = \frac{\sqrt{3}}{2}$ when $\theta = \frac{\pi}{3}$ and when $\theta = \frac{2\pi}{3}$. Since only $\frac{2\pi}{3}$ is in the given range of $\frac{\pi}{2} < \theta < \pi$, $\theta = \frac{2\pi}{3}$.

9. C: "The square of twice the sum of x and three is equal to the product of twenty-four and x" is represented by the equation $[2(x+3)]^2 = 24x$. Solve for x.

$$[2x + 6]^2 = 24x$$
$$(2x + 6)(2x + 6) = 24x$$
$$4x^2 + 24x + 36 = 24x$$
$$4x^2 + 36 = 0$$
$$4x^2 = -36$$
$$x^2 = -9$$
$$x = \pm\sqrt{-9}$$
$$x = \pm 3i$$

So, $-3i$ is a possible value of x.

10. B: The teacher has explained the commutative property, which is one of the properties of real numbers.

11. A: The set of integers, $\{-3, -2, -1, 0, 1, 2, 3, \dots\}$, does not contain fractions. Since $\frac{1}{4}$ is a rational, real number, it cannot be an irrational number.

12. B: Get as many terms as possible out from the radical and any radicals out from the denominator:

$$\sqrt{\frac{-32x^4}{75y^5}} = \sqrt{\frac{-16x^4 \cdot (2)}{25y^4 \cdot (3y)}}$$
$$= \sqrt{\frac{-(4x^2)^2 \cdot (2)}{(5y^2)^2 \cdot (3y)}}$$
$$= \frac{4x^2 i\sqrt{2}}{5y^2\sqrt{3y}} \cdot \frac{\sqrt{3y}}{\sqrt{3y}}$$
$$= \frac{4x^2 i\sqrt{6y}}{15y^3}$$

13. B: If each number is rounded to the nearest thousand, 15,012 rounds to 15,000, and 19,938 rounds to 20,000. We would therefore expect $\frac{15{,}012}{19{,}938}$ to be close to $\frac{15{,}000}{20{,}000}$, which can be simplified to $\frac{15{,}000 \div 1{,}000}{20{,}000 \div 1{,}000} = \frac{15}{20} = \frac{15 \div 5}{20 \div 5} = \frac{3}{4}$.

14. D: Since the graph shows a maximum height of 24 inches above the ground, and since the maximum distance from the road the pebble reaches occurs when it is at the top of the tire, the diameter of the tire is 24 inches. Therefore, its radius is 12 inches. From the graph, it can be observed that the tire makes 6 rotations in 2 seconds. Thus, the tire rotates 3 times in 1 second, or $3 \times 60 = 180$ times per minute.

15. D: If the distance is 2.5 cm on the map, then the actual distance is 2.5 cm $\times \frac{20 \text{ m}}{1 \text{ cm}} = 50$ m. To find x, use the Pythagorean theorem, then solve the resulting quadratic equation.

$$x^2 + (x - 10)^2 = (50)^2$$
$$x^2 + x^2 - 20x + 100 = 2{,}500$$
$$2x^2 - 20x - 2{,}400 = 0$$
$$2(x^2 - 10x - 1{,}200) = 0$$
$$2(x - 40)(x + 30) = 0$$
$$x = 40 \quad x = -30$$

Since x represents a distance, it cannot be –30, so $x = 40$. Juan walks a total of $(40 - 10) + 40 = 70$ m to get to the park.

16. C: Since there are 100 cm in a meter, on a 1: 150 scale drawing, each centimeter represents 1.5 m. Therefore, an area of one square centimeter on the drawing represents 2.25 square meters in the real room. Since the area of the room in the scale drawing is 20 cm^2, the room's actual area is 45 m^2.

Another way to determine the area of the room is to write and solve an equation using the area formula for a rectangle.

$\frac{l}{150} \times \frac{w}{150} = 20 \text{ cm}^2$, where l and w are the dimensions of the actual room:

$$\frac{lw}{22{,}500} = 20 \text{ cm}^2$$

$$\text{Area} = 450{,}000 \text{ cm}^2$$

Since this is not one of the answer choices, convert cm^2 to m^2:

$$450{,}000 \text{ cm}^2 \times \frac{1 \text{ m}}{100 \text{ cm}} \times \frac{1 \text{ m}}{100 \text{ cm}} = 45 \text{ m}^2$$

17. C: The movement of the weight can be described by graphing height h in inches as a function of time t in seconds. Notice that the height is 4.5 in above the table at time 0 since the weight was pulled down 1.5 inches from its starting position 6 inches above the table. The spring fluctuates 1.5 inches above and below its equilibrium point, so its maximum height is 7.5 inches above the table. The graph represents a cosine curve that has been inverted, stretched vertically by a factor of 1.5, and shifted up 6 units; also, the graph has been compressed horizontally, with a period of 0.5 rather than 2π. So, the height of the weight on the spring as a function of time is $h = -1.5\cos(4\pi t) + 6$.

18. B: First, square the binomial.

$$(3 - 2i)^2 + (7 + 7i) = 9 - 12i + 4i^2 + 7 + 7i$$

Then, simplify $i^2 = -1$.

$$9 - 12i - 4 + 7 + 7i$$

Finally, combine like terms.

$$12 - 5i$$

19. C: Sketch a diagram and label the known segments. Use the property that two segments are congruent when they originate from the same point outside of a circle and are tangent to the circle. The point of tangency of $\overline{CD}$ divides the segment into two pieces measuring 4 and 4. The point of tangency of $\overline{BC}$ divides the segment into two pieces measuring 4 and 8; the point of tangency of $\overline{AB}$ divides the segment into two pieces measuring 2 and 8. Finally, the point of tangency of $\overline{AD}$ divides the segment into two pieces measuring 2 and 4. Therefore, $\overline{AD} = 2 + 4 = 6$.

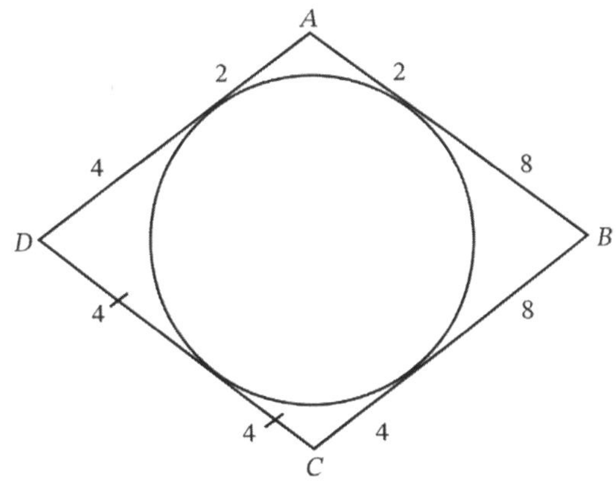

20. B: To solve the equation, write $x^4 + 64 = 20x^2$ in the quadratic form, then factor.

$$(x^2)^2 - 20(x^2) + 64 = 0$$

This trinomial can be factored as $(x^2 - 4)(x^2 - 16) = 0$. Each set of parentheses contains a difference of squares, which can be factored further: $(x + 2)(x - 2)(x + 4)(x - 4) = 0$. Use the zero product property to find the solutions to the equation.

$x + 2 = 0$	$x - 2 = 0$	$x + 4 = 0$	$x - 4 = 0$
$x = -2$	$x = 2$	$x = -4$	$x = 4$

Therefore, the solution to the equation is $x = \{-4, -2, 2, 4\}$.

21. A: The given values make the Pythagorean theorem true, that is $5^2 + 12^2 = 13^2$. So, this is a right triangle. Let the base of the triangle be $5x$ and the height of the triangle be $12x$. So, the area is $A = \frac{1}{2}bh$, or $\frac{1}{2}(5x)(12x) = 30x^2$.

22. D: The symbol $\wedge$ is the logical conjunction symbol. In order for statement $(p\wedge q)$ to be true, both statements p and q must be true. The $\neg$ symbol means "not," so if $(p\wedge q)$ is true, then $\neg(p\wedge q)$ is false, and if $(p\wedge q)$ is false, then $\neg(p\wedge q)$ is true. The statement $q \leftrightarrow \neg(p\wedge q)$ is true when the value of q is the same as the value of $\neg(p\wedge q)$.

p	q	$(p\wedge q)$	$\neg(p\wedge q)$	$q \leftrightarrow \neg(p\wedge q)$
T	T	T	F	F
T	F	F	T	F
F	T	F	T	T

p	q	$(p \wedge q)$	$\neg(p \wedge q)$	$q \leftrightarrow \neg(p \wedge q)$
F	F	F	T	F

23. B: Authentic assessment techniques are designed to build higher-order thinking skills because they require students to construct their own answers instead of choosing from preselected answers. They also allow for the possibility that multiple "correct" answers are possible because students bring different perspectives and prior experiences to the material. They typically measure student performance over an extended period of time and are graded on a criterion-referenced basis (e.g., students are compared to an objective standard, rather than being directly compared to one another).

24. B: Use the table of values to first write equations for $f(x)$ and $g(x)$: $f(x) = 2x^3$ and $g(x) = 3x - 5$. Then, use those equations to find $f(g(3))$.

$$g(3) = 3(3) - 5 = 9 - 5 = 4$$
$$f(4) = 2(4)^3 = 2(64) = 128$$

So, $f\big(g(3)\big) = f(4) = 128$.

25. B: The area of a triangle is $A = \frac{1}{2}bh$, where b and h are the lengths of the triangle's base and height, respectively. The base of the given triangle is x, but the height is not given. Since the triangle is a right triangle and the hypotenuse is given, the triangle's height can be found using the Pythagorean theorem.

$$x^2 + h^2 = 6^2$$
$$h = \sqrt{36 - x^2}$$

To find the area of the triangle in terms of x, substitute $\sqrt{36 - x^2}$ for the height and x for the base of the triangle into the area formula $\left(A = \frac{1}{2}bh\right)$:

$$A(x) = \frac{1}{2}(x)(\sqrt{36 - x^2})$$
$$A(x) = \frac{x\sqrt{36 - x^2}}{2}$$

26. D: The graph of $f(x)$ is stretched vertically by a factor of 2 and is inverted with respect to $y = \sin x$, so $a_1 = -2$. The graph of $g(x)$ is stretched vertically by a factor of 4 with respect to the graph of $y = \cos x$, so $a_2 = 4$. Therefore, the statement $a_1 < 0 < a_2$ is true.

27. A: The recursive definition gives the first term of the sequence, $a_1 = -1$. Each term afterward is the sum of the previous term and 2. So the second term is $-1 + 2 = 1$, the third term is $1 + 2 = 3$, and so on.

n	a_n
1	-1
2	1
3	3

The relationship between n and a_n is linear, so the equation of the sequence can be found in the same way as the equation of a line. The value of a_n increases by 2 each time the value of n increases by 1.

n	$2n$	a_n
1	2	-1
2	4	1
3	6	3

Since the difference between $2n$ and a_n is 3, $a_n = 2n - 3$.

n	$2n - 3$	a_n
1	$2 - 3 = -1$	-1
2	$4 - 3 = 1$	1
3	$6 - 3 = 3$	3

28. C: Leonhard Euler made many important contributions to the field of mathematics. This includes the formula for calculating the number of vertices, edges, and faces on a geometric solid.

29. A: In the range $(-\infty, -1)$, the graph represented is $y = 2x - 1$. In the range $[-1,2)$, the graph is $y = -1$. In the range $[2, \infty)$, the graph is $y = -\frac{1}{2}x + 5$.

30. D: Since it is given that $\overline{FD} \cong \overline{BC}$ and $\overline{AB} \cong \overline{DE}$, step 2 needs to establish either that $\overline{AC} \cong \overline{EF}$ or that $\Delta ABC \cong \Delta FDE$ in order for step 5 to show that $\Delta ABC \cong \Delta EDF$. The statement $\overline{AC} \cong \overline{EF}$ cannot be shown directly from the given information. On the other hand, $\Delta ABC \cong \Delta FDE$ can be determined: when two parallel lines $\overline{BC} \parallel \overline{FG}$ are cut by a transversal ($\overline{AE}$), alternate exterior angles (ΔABC, ΔFDE) are congruent. Therefore, $\Delta ABC \cong \Delta EDF$ by the side-angle-side (SAS) theorem.

31. A: Step 5 established that $\Delta ABC \cong \Delta EDF$. Because corresponding parts of congruent triangles are congruent (CPCTC), $\angle BAC \cong \angle DEF$. This is useful to establish when trying to prove $\overline{FE} \parallel \overline{AG}$: when two lines ($\overline{FE}$ and $\overline{AG}$) are cut by a transversal ($\overline{AE}$) and alternate interior angles ($\angle BAC$, $\angle DEF$) are congruent, then the lines are parallel. The completed proof is shown below:

Statement	Reason
1. $\overline{BC} \parallel \overline{FG}$	Given
2. $\angle ABC \cong \angle FDE$	Alternate exterior angles of parallel lines are congruent

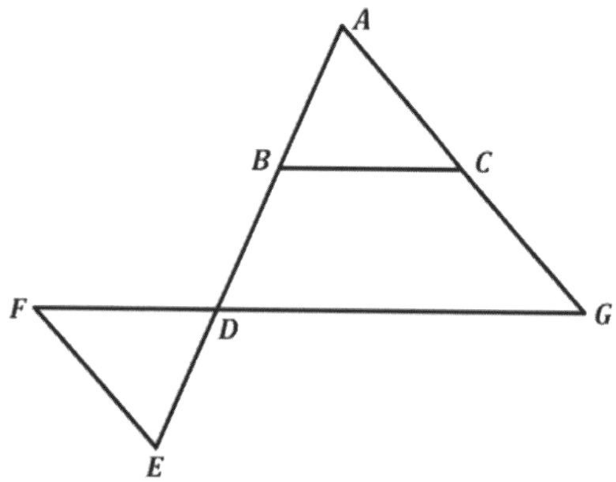

Given: $\overline{BC} \parallel \overline{FG}$; $\overline{FD} \cong \overline{BC}$; $\overline{AB} \cong \overline{DE}$
Prove: $\overline{FE} \parallel \overline{AG}$

Statement	Reason
3. $\overline{FD} \cong \overline{BC}$	Given
4. $\overline{AB} \cong \overline{DE}$	Given
5. $\Delta ABC \cong \Delta EDF$	SAS
6. $\angle BAC \cong \angle DEF$	CPCTC
7. $\overline{FE} \parallel \overline{AG}$	Alternate interior angles congruent then lines are parallel

■

32. D: Students need to learn and practice computation skills, but they also need to learn that the mathematical skills they acquire in the classroom have practical value in their lives outside of school.

33. C: The Babylonians used a base-60 numeral system, which is still used in the division of an hour into 60 minutes, a minute into 60 seconds, and a circle into 360 degrees. The word "algebra" and its development as a discipline separate from geometry are attributed to the Arabic/Islamic civilization. The Greek philosopher Thales is credited with using deductive reasoning to prove geometric concepts. Boolean logic was introduced by British mathematician George Boole.

34. D: Use trigonometric equalities and identities to rewrite the expression. First, convert $\tan\theta$ to $\frac{\sin\theta}{\cos\theta}$.

$$\sin\theta\tan\theta$$

$$\sin\theta \times \frac{\sin\theta}{\cos\theta}$$

From here, multiply the two values.

$$\frac{\sin^2\theta}{\cos\theta}$$

Use the trigonometric identity $\sin^2\theta = 1 - \cos^2\theta$.

$$\frac{1-\cos^2\theta}{\cos\theta}$$

Then, separate the fractions into two separate fractions.

$$\frac{1}{\cos\theta} - \frac{\cos^2\theta}{\cos\theta}$$

$$\frac{1}{\cos\theta} - \cos\theta$$

Finally, convert $\frac{1}{\cos\theta}$ to $\sec\theta$.

$$\sec\theta - \cos\theta$$

35. C: In a parallelogram, consecutive angles are supplementary; that is, the sum of their measures is 180°. Use this to write an equation and then solve for x.

$$\begin{aligned} m\angle A + m\angle B &= 180^\circ \\ (5x) + (2x - 9) &= 180 \\ 7x - 9 &= 180 \\ 7x &= 189 \\ x &= 27 \end{aligned}$$

In a parallelogram, opposite angles are congruent. Thus, $m\angle B = m\angle C$, so find the value of $m\angle B$.

$$\begin{aligned} m\angle B &= 2x - 9 \\ &= 2(27) - 9 \\ &= 45^\circ \end{aligned}$$

Therefore, $m\angle C = 45^\circ$.

36. D: The student's work contains an error regarding the multiplication process. The student has multiplied the numerators by the incorrect amount. The numerator in $\frac{3}{7}$ should be multiplied by 9, not 7. The numerator in $\frac{4}{9}$ should be multiplied by 7, not 9. This error resulted in an incorrect final answer.

37. D: Adding zero. Adding zero does not assist students in understanding subtraction. Physically taking some objects away from an array of objects, working a problem with a missing addend like $7 + \_\_ = 13$ helps students learn that $13 - 7 = 6$. Moving to the left on a number line is another way of helping students understand subtraction.

38. B: The graph of $f(x)$ is a parabola with a focus of (a, b) and a directrix of $y = -b$. The axis of symmetry of a parabola passes through the focus and vertex and is perpendicular to the directrix. Since the directrix is a horizontal line, the axis of symmetry is $x = a$; therefore, the x-coordinate of the parabola's vertex must be a. The distance between a point on the parabola and the directrix is equal to the distance between that point and the focus, so the y-coordinate of the vertex must be $y = \frac{-b+b}{2} = 0$. So, the vertex of the parabola given by $f(x)$ is $(a, 0)$.

If $g(x)$ were a translation of $f(x)$, as is the case for choices B, C, and D, the vertices of $f(x)$ and $g(x)$ would differ. Since the vertex of the graph of $g(x)$ is $(a, 0)$, none of those choices represent the correct response. However, if $g(x) = -f(x)$, the vertices of the graphs of both functions would be the same; therefore, this represents a possible relation between the two functions.

39. D: There are three possibilities for being homozygous: aa, bb, or cc. We add the numbers for each of these and divide by 1,000 to find the probability that a person in this group is homozygous for one of the alleles:

$$\frac{136 + 213 + 180}{1{,}000} = \frac{529}{1{,}000} = 0.529$$

Multiply this experimental probability by 10,000 to find the number of individuals expected to be homozygous for any of the alleles in a population of 10,000: $0.529 \times 10{,}000 = 5{,}290$.

40. B: A line graph is often used to show change over time. A Venn diagram shows the relationships among sets. A box-and-whisker plot displays how numeric data are distributed throughout the range. A pie chart shows the relationship of parts to a whole.

41. D: For the Final, the third quartile is 87. Since 75% of the data in a set is below the third quartile, there is a 75% chance, or a probability of 0.75, that a test score chosen at random from the Final scored below 87.

42. C: We calculate volume of a cylinder with the following formula: $V = \pi r^2 h$, where r is the radius and h is the height. The radius is half of the given diameter, or 420 in, so $V = \pi(420)^2(220) =$ 121,857,120. We can write this in scientific notation by moving the decimal to the left 8 places: $1.22x10^8$ in^3. Answer A is the area of the base of the water tower. Answer B is the surface area of the water tower. Answer D is the volume using the value of the diameter as the radius.

43. A: The student could use (3 × 75) ÷ 5 to solve this problem. Answer choice A could be expressed 3/5 × 75/1, which simplifies to (3 × 75)/5 = 225/5 = 45. The answer then is that 3/5 of 75 is 45.

44. B: One way to approach this problem is to first consider the number of arrangements of the five members of the family if Tasha (T) and Mac (M) must sit together. Treat them as a unit seated in a fixed location at the table; then arrange the other three family members (A, B, and C):

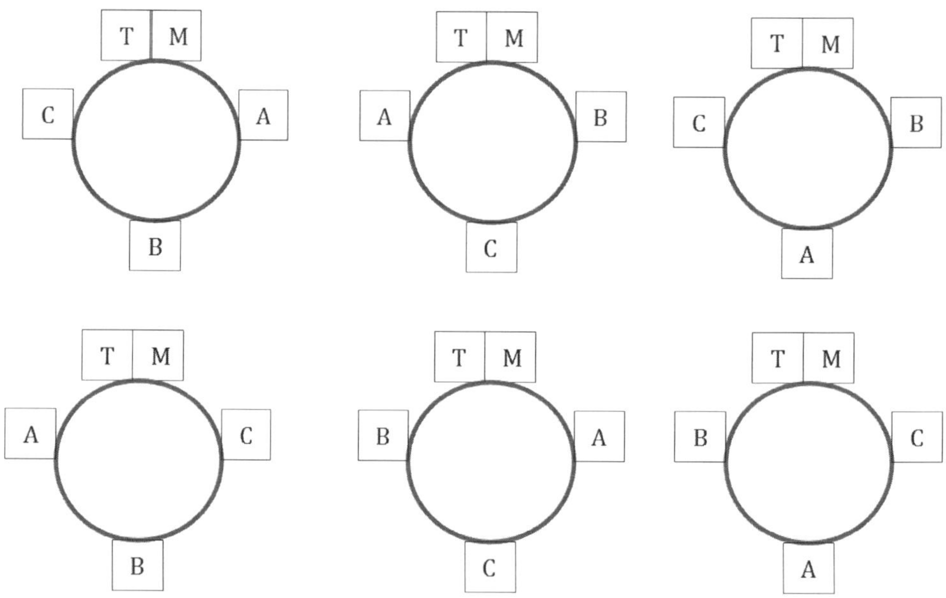

There are six ways to arrange four units around a circle as shown. Any other arrangement would be a rotation in which the elements are in the same order and would therefore not be a unique arrangement. Of course, Mac and Tasha are not actually a single unit. They would still be sitting beside each other if they were to trade seats, so there are 12 arrangements in which the two are seated next to one another. In all other arrangements of the five family members, they are separated. Therefore, to find the number of arrangements in which Tasha and Mac are *not* sitting together, subtract 12 from the possible arrangement of five units around a circle. There are $(n-1)!$ ways to arrange n units around a circle for $n > 1$. So, $(5-1)! - 12 = 24 - 12 = 12$.

45. B: Coins would be the simplest way to compare all the provided numbers, as it would be more difficult to divide play clay or interlocking cubes into 100 parts or to draw and color 100 parts.

Students are usually taught coin values before they learn to convert between equivalent decimals, fractions, and percents, so teachers can capitalize on this prior knowledge.

46. A: Percent error $= \frac{|\text{actual value} - \text{measured value}|}{\text{actual value}} \times 100\%$, and the average percent error is the sum of the percent errors for each trial divided by the number of trials.

	Percent Error Trial 1	Percent Error Trial 2	Percent Error Trial 3	Percent Error Trial 4	Average Percent Error
Scale 1	0.4%	0.6%	0.2%	0.6%	0.45%
Scale 2	0.2%	0.2%	0.4%	0.2%	0.25%

The percent error for Scale 2 is less than the percent error for Scale 1, so it is more accurate. The more precise scale is also Scale 2 because its range of values, 4.99 g − 5.02 g = 0.03 g, is smaller than Scale 1's range of values, 4.97 g − 5.03 g = 0.06 g.

47. C: The two functions that combine to form $g(x)$ meet at $x = 2$. The slope is positive to the left of $x = 2$, rising to the intersection point (2,2). The slope is negative to the right of $x = 2$. Thus, while the domain of $g(x)$ is all real numbers because there is an output for every possible x-value, the range is $y \leq 2$. We can find the solution when $x = 1$ by plugging 1 into the bottom equation, since 1 is less than 2. If $g(x) = x$ and $x = 1$, then $g(1) = 1$. So, statements I and II are true, while statement III is false.

48. A: The area of each circle can be found by the formula $A = \pi r^2$. The radius of Circle A is half the diameter, or 6 cm, so the area of Circle A is $\pi(6)^2 = 36\pi$. The radius of Circle B is 15 cm, so the area of Circle B is $\pi(15)^2 = 225\pi$. The ratio of Circle A to Circle B is $\frac{36\pi}{225\pi} = \frac{36}{225} = \frac{4}{25}$. Answer B is the ratio of the areas of the two circles if both given measurements are treated as the diameter or as the radius, rather than one of each. Answer C is the ratio of the circumferences of the two circles. Answer D is the ratio of the circumferences of the two circles if both given measurements are treated as the diameter or as the radius, rather than one of each.

49. B: This is the graph of the parent function $y = \sqrt{x}$. Another way to determine the function is by testing points. Notice that the graph passes through the points (0,0), and (4,2). A quick check of each x-value shows that the only function that produces y-values of 0 and 2 is $y = \sqrt{x}$.

x	x^2	$\sqrt{x}$	2^x	$\log_2 x$
0	0	0	1	undefined
4	16	2	16	2

50. B: If the statement is written in the form $p \to q$, then the converse is represented as $q \to p$. Thus, the converse should read, "If it is winter, then I go skiing."

51. D: Radioactive decay can be modeled with an exponential function. The path of a sound wave is modeled by a sine or cosine function. The path of a ball being kicked into the air is modeled by a quadratic function. The distance an object travels over time when the rate is constant is modeled by a linear function.

52. C: There are three ways in which two women from the same department can be selected: two women can be selected from Biology, two women can be selected from Chemistry, or two women can be selected from Physics. Since the events of choosing one woman and then another are both independent events, multiply the two probabilities together to get the probability of choosing two women from the same department.

Biology	Chemistry	Physics
$\frac{26}{129} \times \frac{25}{128} = \frac{650}{16{,}512}$	$\frac{31}{129} \times \frac{30}{128} = \frac{930}{16{,}512}$	$\frac{20}{129} \times \frac{19}{128} = \frac{380}{16{,}512}$

Since any of these is a distinct possible outcome, the probability that two women will be selected from the same department is the sum of these outcomes.

$$\frac{650}{16{,}512} + \frac{930}{16{,}512} + \frac{380}{16{,}512} = \frac{1{,}960}{16{,}512} \approx 0.119 = 11.9\%$$

53. D: Set the given expression equal to y, then solve for y. When $y = \frac{1}{\sqrt{x}}$, $x = \frac{1}{y^2}$ or y^{-2}. Similarly, when $y = \cos x$, $x = \cos^{-1} y$. On the other hand, when $y = 2x$, $x = \frac{y}{2}$; when $y = e^x$, $x = \ln y$ for $y > 0$; and when $y = \frac{1}{x^2}$, $x = \pm\sqrt{\frac{1}{y}}$.

54. D: Since a and b are multiples of 6, each can be expressed as the product of 6 and an integer. So, if we write $a = 6x$ and $b = 6y$ then, $3(6x)^2 + 2(6y)^3 = c$. Simplify and factor.

$$3(6x)^2 + 2(6y)^3 = c$$
$$108x^2 + 432y^3 = c$$
$$108(x^2 + 4y^3) = c$$

Since c is the product of 108 and some other integer, 108 must be a factor of c.

55. D: Levi walked 3 miles from home and then back again, so he walked a total of 6 miles. Therefore, statement III is true. He traveled these 6 miles in 6 hours, so his average speed was 1 mph. Therefore, statement I is true. He walked 3 miles from point A to B in 1 hour and 2 miles from E to F in 1 hour, so his speed averaged 3 mph between A and B and 2 mph between E and F. Therefore, statement II is false.

56. B: The average rate of cooling is: (86° - 38°) / 9 hrs; 48° / 9 = 5.33° F per hour.

57. A: The inequality that represents this scenario is $n + 3p \leq 30$, where n is the number of notebooks and p is the number of boxes of pencils. To graph this inequality, find the intercepts of this linear inequality by making the inequality an equality and setting n and p equal to 0 and solving for the other variable.

$$(0) + 3p = 30$$
$$3p = 30$$
$$p = 10$$

$$n + 3(0) = 30$$
$$n = 30$$

The intercepts are $n = 30$ and $p = 10$. The solid line through the two intercepts represents the maximum number of each item that may be purchased. Since this inequality represents the maximum he can purchase, all first-quadrant points below the line are also possible amounts within Ben's budget.

58. B: The side lengths rounded to the nearest ten centimeters are 20 cm, 20 cm, and 10 cm. Then the estimated perimeter is the sum found by adding $20 + 20 + 10 = 50$. The perimeter is about 50 cm.

59. A: Use a Venn diagram to help organize the given information. Start by filling in the space where the three circles intersect: one student enrolled in all three areas. Use that information to fill in the spaces where two circles intersect. For example, seven students are taking both Intro to Law and Latin, and one of those is also taking Biophysics, so six students are taking Intro to Law and Latin but not Biophysics. Once the diagram is completed, add the number of students from each portion of the diagram. The total number of students taking special electives is $12 + 14 + 9 + 3 + 1 + 6 + 1 = 46$.

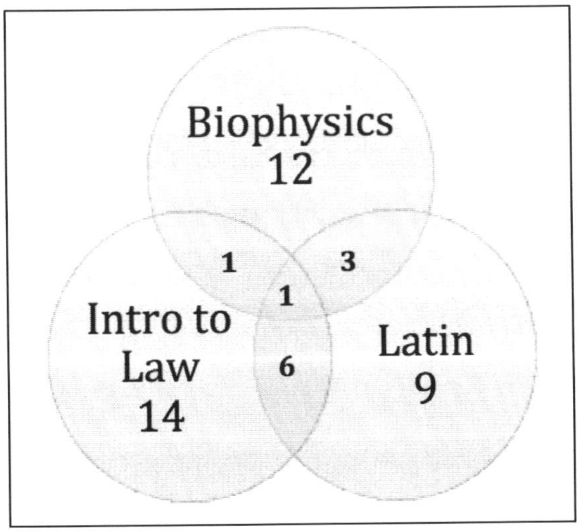

60. C: In this sequence, the interval between successive numbers increases by an amount that is one less than the previous interval.

$$23 - 18 = 5$$
$$27 - 23 = 4$$
$$33 - 32 = 1$$

Therefore, the next number should be $27 + 3$, or 30.

61. C: The expression representing the monthly charge for Company A is $\$25 + \$0.05m$, where m is the time in minutes spent talking on the phone. Set this expression equal to the monthly charge for Company B, which is $50. Solve for m to find the number of minutes the two companies charge the same amount.

$$\$25 + \$0.05m = \$50$$
$$\$0.05m = \$25$$
$$m = 500$$

Notice that the answer choices are given in hours, not in minutes. Since there are 60 minutes in an hour, $m = \frac{500}{60}$ hours $= 8\frac{1}{3}$ hours. One-third of an hour is 20 minutes, so m is 8 hours and 20 minutes.

62. D: First, state the exclusions of the domain.

$$x^3 - 7x + 6 \neq 0$$
$$(x+3)(x-1)(x-2) \neq 0$$
$$x + 3 \neq 0 \quad x - 1 \neq 0 \quad x - 2 \neq 0$$
$$x \neq -3 \qquad x \neq 1 \qquad x \neq 2$$

To determine whether there are asymptotes or holes at these values of x, simplify the expression:

$$\frac{x^2 - x - 2}{x^3 - 7x + 6} = \frac{(x-2)(x+1)}{(x+3)(x-1)(x-2)} = \frac{x+1}{(x+3)(x-1)}$$

There are asymptotes at $x = 1$ and at $x = -3$ and a hole at $x = 2$. Statement I is false.

To find the x-intercept of $f(x)$, solve $f(x) = 0$. $f(x) = 0$ when the numerator is equal to zero. The numerator equals zero when $x = 2$ and $x = -1$; however, 2 is excluded from the domain of $f(x)$, so the x-intercept is -1. This is enough to say statement II is false. To find the y-intercept of $f(x)$, find $f(0)$.

$$f(0) = \frac{0^2 - 0 - 2}{0^3 - 7(0) + 6} = \frac{-2}{6} = -\frac{1}{3}$$

The y-intercept is $-\frac{1}{3}$, but the x-intercept is not $-\frac{1}{3}$. Statement II is false.

63. B: The recursive definition of the sequence gives the first term of the series, $a_1 = 2$. The definition also defines each term in the series as the sum of the previous term and -3. Therefore, the second term in the series is $2 + (-3) = -1$, the third term in the series is $-1 + (-3) = -4$, and so on.

n	a_n
1	2
2	-1
3	-4

The relationship between n and a_n is linear, so the equation of the sequence can be found using the explicit formula for an arithmetic sequence, $a_n = a_1 + d(n-1)$, where a_n is the value of any term n, a_1 is the value of the first term, and d is the common difference between each term. The value of a_n decreases by 3 each time the value of n increases by 1, so the common difference (d) is -3.

Substitute all the known values into the equation for the explicit formula for an arithmetic sequence, and simplify the formula.

$$a_n = 2 + (-3)(n-1)$$
$$a_n = 2 - 3n + 3$$
$$a_n = -3n + 5$$

64. A: A system of linear equations can be solved by using matrices or by using the graphing, substitution, or elimination method. The elimination method is shown here.

$$\begin{cases} 3x + y = 1 \\ -4x + 3y = 29 \end{cases}$$

To eliminate y by the elimination method, multiply the top equation by –3 so that the coefficients of the y-terms will be additive inverses.

$$-3(3x + y) = (1)(-3)$$
$$-9x - 3y = -3$$

Then, add the two equations and solve for x.

$$\begin{array}{rrcl} & -9x \ -3y & = & -3 \\ + & -4x \ +3y & = & 29 \\ \hline & -13x & = & 26 \\ & x & = & -2 \end{array}$$

Substitute –2 for x in either of the given equations and solve for y. Here $x = -2$ is substituted into the top equation.

$$3(-2) + y = 1$$
$$-6 + y = 1$$
$$y = 7$$

The solution to the system of equations is $(-2, 7)$.

65. A: The critical points of the graph occur when $f'(x) = 0$.

$f(x) = 4x^3 - x^2 - 4x + 2$	
$f'(x) = 12x^2 - 2x - 4$	Take the derivative of $f(x)$.
$f'(x) = 2(6x^2 - x - 2)$	Factor a 2 out of each term in $f'(x)$.
$f'(x) = 2(3x - 2)(2x + 1)$	Factor the new polynomial in $f'(x)$.
$0 = 2(3x - 2)(2x + 1)$	Set $f'(x)$ equal to 0.
$3x - 2 = 0$ $x = \frac{2}{3}$	Solve the first factor to find the value of x that makes it 0.
$2x + 1 = 0$ $x = -\frac{1}{2}$	Solve the second factor to find the value of x that makes it 0.

The critical points of the graph are at $x = \frac{2}{3}$ and $x = -\frac{1}{2}$.

To determine if these points are relative maximums or minimums, test points on each end of the intervals surrounding them. Start by testing a point less than $-\frac{1}{2}$. For example, solve for the value of $f'(x)$ when $x = -1$.

$$f'(-1) = 12(-1)^2 - 2(-1) - 4 = 12 + 2 - 4 = 10$$

Now, test a point greater than $-\frac{1}{2}$ and less than $\frac{2}{3}$, like 0.

$$f'(0) = 12(0)^2 - 2(0) - 4 = 0 - 0 - 4 = -4$$

Therefore, when $x < -\frac{1}{2}$, $f'(x) > 0$, and when $-\frac{1}{2} < x < \frac{2}{3}$, $f'(x) < 0$, so the point where $x = -\frac{1}{2}$ is a relative maximum of the function. Now, test a point greater than $\frac{2}{3}$, like 1.

$$f'(1) = 12(1)^2 - 2(1) - 4 = 12 - 2 - 4 = 6$$

When $x > \frac{2}{3}$, $f'(x) > 0$, so the point where $x = \frac{2}{3}$ is a relative minimum. To find the corresponding y-values for these points, substitute each value of x into the original function and solve for y.

If $f''(x) > 0$ for all x in an interval, the graph of the function is concave upward on that interval, and if $f''(x) < 0$ for all x in an interval, the graph of the function is concave downward on that interval. Find the second derivative of the function and determine the intervals in which $f''(x)$ is less than zero and greater than zero.

$$f''(x) = 24x - 2$$

$$\begin{array}{rr} 24x - 2 < 0 & \quad 24x - 2 > 0 \\ x < \dfrac{1}{12} & \quad x > \dfrac{1}{12} \end{array}$$

The graph of f is concave downward on the interval $\left(-\infty, \frac{1}{12}\right)$ and concave upward on the interval $\left(\frac{1}{12}, \infty\right)$.

66. B: A score of 91 is one standard deviation above the mean ($84 + 7 = 91$). Since approximately 68% of the data is within one standard deviation of the mean, about 32% (100% − 68%) of the data is outside of one standard deviation within the mean. Normally distributed data is symmetric about the mean, which means that about 16% of the data lies below one standard deviation below the mean and about 16% of data lies above one standard deviation above the mean. Therefore, approximately 16% of the students scored 91 or higher. Since 16% of 250 is 40, about 40 students scored at least 91.

67. C: The situation may be modeled by the system of inequalities $\begin{cases} 6x + 3y \leq 75 \\ x + y \leq 30 \end{cases}$ where x is the number of coffee mugs and y is the number of note pads. Some algebraic manipulation gives us the inequalities in slope-intercept form: $\begin{cases} y \leq -2x + 25 \\ y \leq -x + 30 \end{cases}$. All four choices graph these lines correctly, but only choice C correctly shades just the region that is below both lines, indicating that both conditions are met.

68. D: There are many ways Josephine may have applied her knowledge to determine how to approximately measure her medicine using her plastic spoon. The expression below shows how she converts from cubic centimeters to spoons.

$$25\text{ cc} \times \frac{1\text{ mL}}{1\text{ cc}} \times \frac{1\text{L}}{1{,}000\text{ mL}} \times \frac{0.5\text{ gal}}{2\text{ L}} \times \frac{16\text{ c}}{1\text{ gal}} \times \frac{48\text{ t}}{1\text{ c}} \times \frac{1\text{ spoonful}}{1\text{ t}}$$

$$\frac{25}{1{,}000} \times \frac{1}{4} \times 16 \times 48$$

The only choice which correctly uses dimensional analysis is choice D.

69. D: First, apply the laws of exponents to simplify the expression on the left. Then, add the two fractions.

$\frac{(x^2y^{-3})(4xy)^2}{16x^4y^4} + \frac{3}{2xy}$	Write out the original expression.
$\frac{(x^2y^{-3})(16x^2y^2)}{16x^4y^4} + \frac{3}{2xy}$	Simplify the squared term in the left fraction's numerator.
$\frac{16x^4y^{-1}}{16x^4y^4} + \frac{3}{2xy}$	Multiply the two monomials in the left fraction's numerator using the exponent rule $x^m \cdot x^n = x^{m+n}$.
$\frac{1}{y^5} + \frac{3}{2xy}$	Simplify the left fraction using the exponent rule $\frac{x^m}{x^n} = x^{m-n}$ and the rule $x^{-n} = \frac{1}{x^n}$.
$\frac{1}{y^5} \cdot \frac{2x}{2x} + \frac{3}{2xy} \cdot \frac{y^4}{y^4}$	Create common denominators between the two fractions by multiplying them each by a factor of 1.
$\frac{2x}{2xy^5} + \frac{3y^4}{2xy^5}$	Simplify the multiplication.
$\frac{2x + 3y^4}{2xy^5}$	Add the two fractions.

70. A: One way to find an inverse function is to take the original equation describing the function, replace $f(x)$ with x and x with $f^{-1}(x)$, and then solve for $f^{-1}(x)$. In this case, $f(x) = \tan(2x + 4)$ becomes $x = \tan(2f^{-1}(x) + 4)$. To solve for $f^{-1}(x)$, first take the inverse tangent of both sides: $\tan^{-1} x = \tan^{-1}(\tan(2f^{-1}(x) + 4)) = 2f^{-1}(x) + 4$. Now subtract four from both sides: $\tan^{-1} x - 4 = 2f^{-1}(x)$. Finally, divide both sides by 2: $\frac{1}{2}(\tan^{-1} x - 4) = f^{-1}(x)$, or $f^{-1}(x) = \frac{1}{2}\tan^{-1} x - 2$.

71. A: In this sequence, each number is either double the preceding number or 2 more than the preceding number, and these procedures alternate. Since $36 = 2 \times 18$, the next element of the sequence will be determined by adding 2. Since $36 + 2 = 38$, the next number in the sequence is 38.

72. C: Multiply the second equation by 2 and combine it with the first equation to eliminate y.

$$\begin{array}{rrrrcr} & 2x & -4y & +1z & = & 10 \\ + & -6x & +4y & -8z & = & -14 \\ \hline & -4x & & -7z & = & -4 \end{array}$$

Multiply the third equation by –2 and combine it with the original second equation to eliminate y.

$$\begin{array}{rrrrcr} & -3x & +2y & -4z & = & -7 \\ + & -2x & -2y & +6z & = & 2 \\ \hline & -5x & & +2z & = & -5 \end{array}$$

Multiply the equation from step one by 5 and the equation from step two by –4 and combine to eliminate x.

$$\begin{array}{rrcl} & -20x\ -35z & = & -20 \\ + & 20x\ -\ 8z & = & 20 \\ \hline & -43z & = & 0 \\ & z & = & 0 \end{array}$$

Substitute 0 for z in the equation from step 2 to find x.

$$\begin{aligned} -5x + 2(0) &= -5 \\ -5x &= -5 \\ x &= 1 \end{aligned}$$

Substitute 0 for z and 1 for x into the first original equation to find y.

$$\begin{aligned} 2(1) - 4y + (0) &= 10 \\ 2 - 4y &= 10 \\ -4y &= 8 \\ y &= -2 \end{aligned}$$

Therefore, the solution to the system of equations is $(1, -2, 0)$.

73. C: A pie chart shows the relationship of parts to a whole. A line graph is often used to show change over time. A box-and-whisker plot displays how numeric data are distributed throughout the range. Box-and-whisker plot is the correct answer. A Venn diagram shows the relationships among sets.

74. B: The most straightforward way of solving this problem is to take advantage of the double-angle formula, $\sin 2x = 2\sin x \cos x$.

$$\begin{aligned} \sin 2x \sec x &= 2\sin x \cos x \sec x \\ &= 2\sin x \cos x \left(\frac{1}{\cos x}\right) \\ &= 2\sin x \end{aligned}$$

75. A: Since all of the answer choices are parallelograms, determine whether the parallelogram is also a rhombus or a rectangle or a square. One way to do this is by examining the parallelogram's diagonals. If the parallelogram's diagonals are perpendicular, then the parallelogram is a rhombus. If the parallelogram's diagonals are congruent, then the parallelogram is a rectangle. If a parallelogram is both a rhombus and a rectangle, then it is a square. To determine whether the diagonals are perpendicular, find the slopes of the diagonals of the quadrilateral.

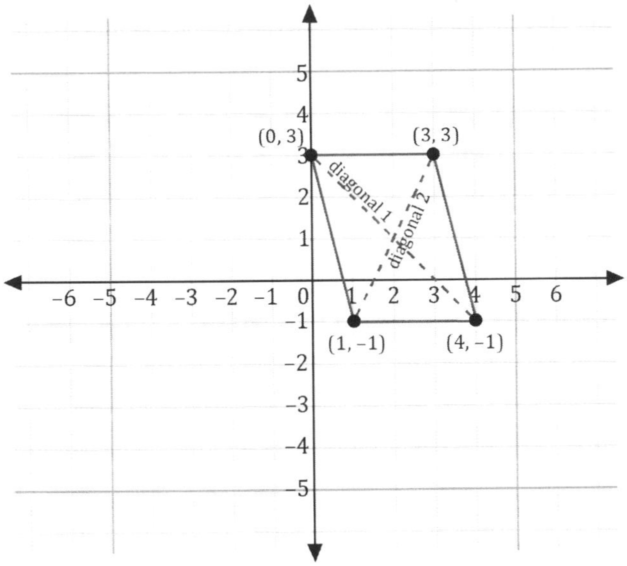

Diagonal 1	Diagonal 2
$\dfrac{-1-3}{4-0} = \dfrac{-4}{4} = -1$	$\dfrac{3-(-1)}{3-1} = \dfrac{4}{2} = 2$

The diagonals do not have opposite reciprocal slopes, so they are not perpendicular. Thus, the parallelogram is *not* a rhombus or a square. To determine whether the diagonals are congruent, find the lengths of the diagonals of the quadrilateral:

Diagonal 1

$$\begin{aligned}\sqrt{(4-0)^2+(-1-3)^2} &= \sqrt{(4)^2+(-4)^2}\\ &= \sqrt{16+16}\\ &= \sqrt{32}\end{aligned}$$

Diagonal 2

$$\begin{aligned}\sqrt{(3-1)^2+(3-(-1))^2} &= \sqrt{(2)^2+(4)^2}\\ &= \sqrt{4+16}\\ &= \sqrt{20}\end{aligned}$$

The diagonals are not congruent, so the parallelogram is not a rectangle. The polygon must be a parallelogram.

76. C: When the dress is marked down by 20%, the cost of the dress is 80% of its original price. Since a percentage can be written as a fraction by placing the percentage over 100, the reduced price of the dress can be written as $\frac{80}{100}x$, or $\frac{4}{5}x$, where x is the original price. When discounted an extra 25%, the dress costs 75% of the reduced price. This results in the expression $\frac{75}{100}\left(\frac{4}{5}x\right)$, which can be simplified to $\frac{3}{4}\left(\frac{4}{5}x\right)$, or $\frac{3}{5}x$. So the final price of the dress is three-fifths of the original price.

77. D: Since the midterm has a low outlier, this skews and decreases the mean for the data set. Therefore, it is not the best reflection of student performance at the midterm. The median would be more accurate. The line in the middle of the box represents the median of the data set, so the median for assessment 2 and the final is the same, not necessarily the mean. Looking at the middle lines of the four boxes, the highest median grades happened with assessment 2 and the final. Since there is a high outlier for assessment 2, this skews the mean higher, meaning it will be greater than the median for this test. Therefore, choice D is correct.

78. C: Substitute and simplify:

$$\begin{aligned}(g \circ f)(x) &= g(f(x)) \\ &= g(3x-2) \\ &= (3x-2)^2 - (3x-2) - 6 \\ &= 9x^2 - 12x + 4 - 3x + 2 - 6 \\ &= 9x^2 - 15x\end{aligned}$$

79. A: This problem is most easily solved using the law of sines, which states that the ratio of the sine of each angle in a triangle to the length of the opposite side is equal: $\frac{\sin A}{a} = \frac{\sin B}{b} = \frac{\sin C}{c}$. In this case, angle θ is opposite side a, and the angle with a measure of 30° is opposite side b, so we can write $\frac{\sin\theta}{a} = \frac{\sin 30°}{b}$. Since $\sin 30° = \frac{1}{2}$, this becomes $\frac{\sin\theta}{a} = \frac{\frac{1}{2}}{b}$, or $\sin\theta = \frac{a}{2b}$.

80. C: The x-intercept is the point at which $f(x) = 0$. When $0 = \log_b x$, $b^0 = x$; since $b^0 = 1$, the x-intercept of $f(x) = \log_b x$ is always 1. If $f(x) = \log_b x$ and $x = b$, then $f(x) = \log_b b$, which is, by definition, 1 ($b^1 = b$). If $g(x) = b^x$, then $f(x)$ and $g(x)$ are inverse functions and are therefore symmetric with respect to $y = x$. The statement choice C is not necessarily true since $x < 1$ includes numbers between 0 and 1. The function is undefined when $x < 0$, but not necessarily for $0 < x < 1$.

81. C: The center of the sphere is shared by the center of the cube, and each of the corners of the cube touches the surface of the sphere. Therefore, the diameter of the sphere is the line that passes through the center of the cube and connects one corner of the cube to the opposite corner. In the illustration below, notice that the diameter d of the sphere can be represented as the hypotenuse of a right triangle with a short leg measuring 4 units. (Since the volume of the cube is 64 cubic units, each of its sides measures $\sqrt[3]{64} = 4$ units.) The long leg of the triangle is the diagonal of the base of the cube.

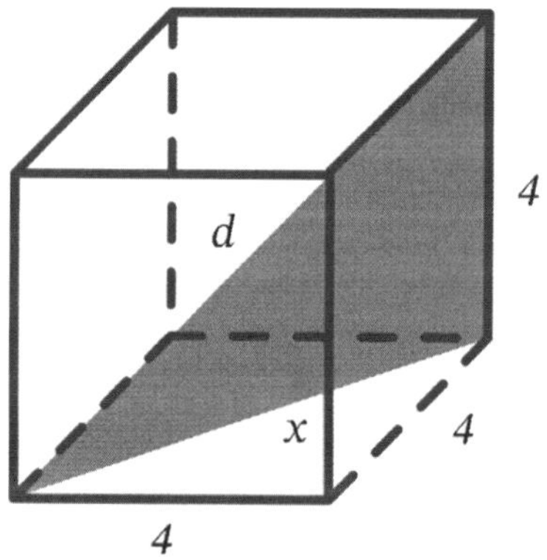

The length of the long leg can be found using the Pythagorean theorem:

$$x^2 = 4^2 + 4^2 = 32$$
$$x = \sqrt{32} = 4\sqrt{2}$$

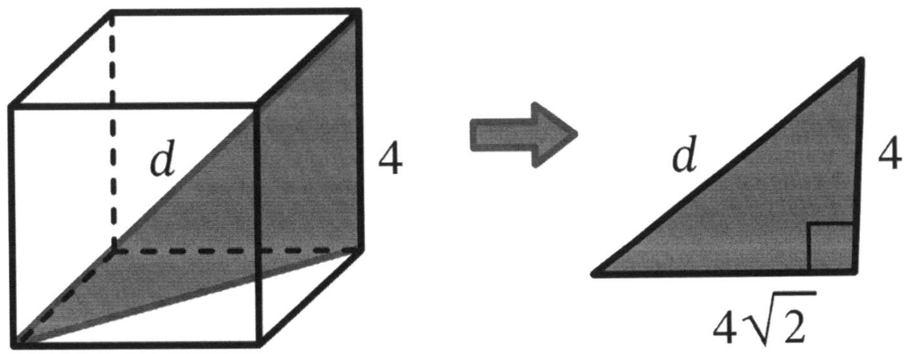

Use the Pythagorean theorem again to find d, the diameter of the sphere:

$$d^2 = \left(4\sqrt{2}\right)^2 + 4^2 = 32 + 16 = 48$$
$$d = \sqrt{48} = 4\sqrt{3}$$

To find the volume of the sphere, use the formula $V = \frac{4}{3}\pi r^3$. Since the radius r of the sphere is half the diameter, $r = 2\sqrt{3}$, and $V = \frac{4}{3}\pi(2\sqrt{3})^3 = \frac{4}{3}\pi\left(24\sqrt{3}\right) = 32\pi\sqrt{3}$ cubic units.

82. B: The only cross-section connecting the points that is not possible is a square; a rectangle is possible, but a square is not.

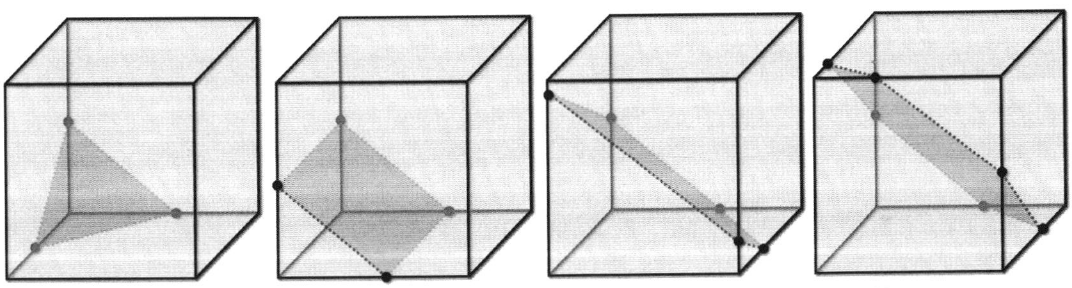

83. C: One way to solve the equation is to write $x^4 + 225 = 34x^2$ in the following form.

$$x^4 - 34x^2 + 225 = 0$$

This trinomial can be factored as $(x^2 - 9)(x^2 - 25) = 0$. In each set of parentheses is a difference of squares, which can be factored further: $(x + 3)(x - 3)(x + 5)(x - 5) = 0$. Use the zero-product property to find the solutions to the equation.

$x + 3 = 0$	$x - 3 = 0$	$x + 5 = 0$	$x - 5 = 0$
$x = -3$	$x = 3$	$x = -5$	$x = 5$

Therefore, the solution to the equation is $x = \{-5, -3, 3, 5\}$.

84. C: To find the probability of rolling an even a certain number of times, use the formula:

$$({}_nC_r)p^r q^{n-r}$$

For example, to find the probability of rolling an even four times out of five rolls with a fair die:

$$({}_n\mathrm{C}_r)p^r q^{n-r} = ({}_5\mathrm{C}_4)(0.5)^4(0.5)^1 = \frac{5!}{1!\,4!}(0.5)^4(0.5)^1 \approx 0.156$$

To find the probability of rolling an even four times with the weighted die:

$$({}_n\mathrm{C}_r)p^r q^{n-r} = ({}_5\mathrm{C}_4)(0.707)^4(0.293)^1 = \frac{5!}{1!\,4!}(0.707)^4(0.293)^1 \approx 0.366$$

The calculated probabilities match those shown in choice C.

85. B: The fact that rubrics combine learning objectives, tasks, guidance to students for performing those tasks, and criteria (A) for evaluating student task performance is an advantage they have as assessment tools. Rubrics use a combined set of criteria to try to make an objective assessment of something that is more subjective, such as a performance or presentation. A rubric is very helpful for grounding the grading of a variety of work that students can turn in, but it still is not as objective as something that uses standard, calculated grades. The fact that the performance levels teachers assign are not as precise as number or letter grades or percentages (B) is a disadvantage. The fact that they are brief in nature (C) is an advantage for both students and teachers. The fact that they are both more concise and clearer than many other assessment tools (D) is another advantage.

86. A: The sum of two vectors is equal to the sum of their components. Using component-wise addition, we get the following vector.

$$v + w = \big((4-3),(3+4)\big) = (1,7)$$

To multiply a vector by a scalar, multiply each component by that scalar. Using component-wise scalar multiplication, we get the following vector.

$$2(1,7) = (2 \times 1, 2 \times 7) = (2,14)$$

87. C: A rectangular prism has six rectangular faces. The arrangement of these faces in a two-dimensional figure is a net of a rectangular prism if the figure can be folded to form a rectangular prism. Choices A, B, and D represent three of the possible nets of a rectangular prism (note that choice D is a cube, which is a type of rectangular prism). Choice C is not a viable net.

88. A: 25% of the data in a set is above the third quartile. Since the third quartile for this set is 86, there is a 25% chance that a student chosen at random from Math scored above an 86.

89. B: The line through the center of the box represents the median. The median test score for English and History is the same, not the mean test score, which makes choice B the correct answer. Note that for Science, the median is a better representation of the data than the mean. There is at least one outlier (a point that lies outside of two standard deviations from the mean), which brings down the average test score. In cases such as this, the mean is not the best measure of central tendency, so choice A is not the correct answer. The median of the History scores is 87, and the 3rd quartile scores for Math is also 87, so choice C is not the answer. The median of the English scores is 86, and based on the spread of data, the mean is lower than the median, so choice D is also not correct.

90. B: On the unit circle, $\sin\theta = \frac{\sqrt{2}}{2}$ when $\theta = \frac{\pi}{4}$ and when $\theta = \frac{3\pi}{4}$. Only $\frac{3\pi}{4}$ fits the condition $\frac{\pi}{2} < \theta < \pi$, so $\theta = \frac{3\pi}{4}$.

91. D: The cross-section is a hexagon.

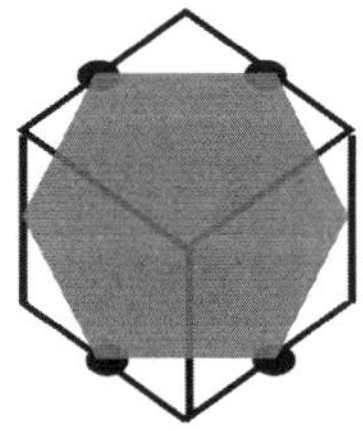

92. B: The endpoint and midpoint of the line segment must lie on the same line. Since we are given the slope of a line and a point on the line, use the point-slope form equation to find the equation of the line.

$$y - y_1 = m(x - x_1)$$
$$y - 3 = -\frac{1}{2}(x - (-2))$$
$$y - 3 = -\frac{1}{2}(x + 2)$$
$$y - 3 = -\frac{1}{2}x - 1$$
$$y = -\frac{1}{2}x + 2$$

From here, substitute the given points into the equation to determine which one is a possible endpoint of the line segment.

a. $(-4, 3)$	b. $(2, 1)$	c. $(-6, 6)$	d. $\left(0, \frac{3}{2}\right)$
$y = -\frac{1}{2}x + 2$	$y = -\frac{1}{2}x + 2$	$y = -\frac{1}{2}x + 2$	$y = -\frac{1}{2}x + 2$
$3 = -\frac{1}{2}(-4) + 2$	$1 = -\frac{1}{2}(2) + 2$	$6 = -\frac{1}{2}(-6) + 2$	$\frac{3}{2} = -\frac{1}{2}(0) + 2$
$3 = 2 + 2$	$1 = -1 + 2$	$6 = 3 + 2$	$\frac{3}{2} = 0 + 2$
$3 = 4$	$1 = 1$	$6 = 5$	$\frac{3}{2} = 2$

The only point that results in a true statement is (2,1), so this is the only point that could be a possible endpoint of the line segment.

93. B: The student's model has no errors. However, his or her interpretation of the model is incorrect. The product of $\frac{1}{3} \times \frac{1}{4}$ is determined by locating the overlapping shaded region. In this case, $\frac{1}{3}$ and $\frac{1}{4}$ overlap on $\frac{1}{12}$ of the model. This means that the product of $\frac{1}{3}$ and $\frac{1}{4}$ is $\frac{1}{12}$. The student's error can be addressed with review of how to interpret models for fraction multiplication.

94. D: One way to determine which is the graph of $f(x) = 2|-x - 1| + 2$ is to find $f(x)$ for a few values of x. For example, $f(0) = 2|0 - 1| + 2 = 4$. Graphs A and D pass through (0,4), but graphs B and C do not. $f(-1) = 2|1 - 1| + 2 = 2$. Graphs B and D pass through $(-1,2)$, but graphs A and C do not. Graph D is the correct graph.

95. B: There are three ways in which two women from the same department can be selected. Two women can be selected from the first department, two women can be selected from the second department, or two women can be selected from the third department.

Department 1	Department 2	Department 3
$\frac{12}{103} \times \frac{11}{102} = \frac{132}{10{,}506}$	$\frac{28}{103} \times \frac{27}{102} = \frac{756}{10{,}506}$	$\frac{16}{103} \times \frac{15}{102} = \frac{240}{10{,}506}$

Since any of these is a distinct possible outcome, the probability that two women will be selected from the same department is the sum of these outcomes.

$$\frac{132}{10{,}506} + \frac{756}{10{,}506} + \frac{240}{10{,}506} = \frac{1{,}128}{10{,}506} \approx 0.107$$

Converting this to a percentage, the probability that two women from the same department will be chosen is approximately 10.7%.

96. B: If l and w represent the length and width of the enclosed area, its perimeter is equal to $2l + 2w$. The fence is positioned x feet from the lot's edges on each side, so the perimeter of the enlarged garden is $2(l + 2x) + 2(w + 2x)$. The extra amount of money spent by fencing the larger area is \$36, and since the fencing material costs \$1.50 per linear foot, 24 more feet of material are used to fence around the garden than would have been used for the original. This can be expressed as the equation:

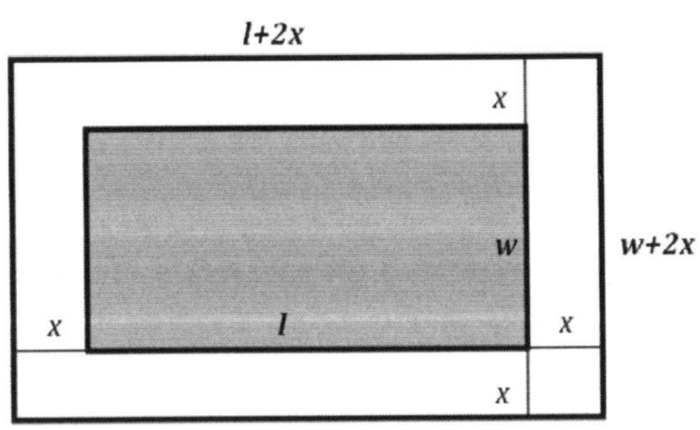

$$\begin{aligned} 2(l + 2x) + 2(w + 2x) - (2l + 2w) &= 24 \\ 2l + 4x + 2w + 4x - 2l - 2w &= 24 \\ 8x &= 24 \\ x &= 3 \end{aligned}$$

This means that Marcus moved the boundary line back 3 feet on each of the four sides. The difference in the area of the lot and the enclosed space is 34 yd^2, which is the same as 306 ft^2. So, $(l + 2x)(w + 2x) - lw = 306$. Substituting 3 for x, we get the following equation and solve.

$$\begin{aligned} (l + 6)(w + 6) - lw &= 306 \\ lw + 6l + 6w + 36 - lw &= 306 \\ 6l + 6w &= 270 \\ 6(l + w) &= 270 \\ l + w &= 45 \end{aligned}$$

Therefore, the length plus the width is equal to 45 feet. This is the original length and width, so we add 6 to each, or 12 total, for a new length and width of 57 feet. Therefore, the perimeter of the enclosed space, $2(l + w)$, is $2(57) = 114$ ft. The cost of 114 ft of chicken wire is $114 \times \$1.50 = \$171$.

97. B: This prompt would help Keisha think of how to keep the ratio the same while still making the right amount of lemonade.

98. A: Besides the \$600 he has remaining, Chan has paid out a total of 85% (30% + 30% + 25%) of his bonus for the expenses described in the question. Therefore, the \$600 represents the remaining 15%. Remember that 15% can be written as $\frac{15}{100}$. To determine his total bonus, solve $\frac{15}{100}x = 600$. So, $x = \frac{100}{15} \times 600 = 4{,}000$, and Chan's total bonus is \$4,000.

99. B: All regular polygons have rotational symmetry. The angle of rotation is the smallest angle by which the polygon can be rotated such that it maps onto itself; any multiple of this angle will also map the polygon onto itself. The angle of rotation for a regular polygon is the angle formed between two lines drawn from consecutive vertices to the center of the polygon. Since the vertices of a regular polygon lie on a circle, for a regular polygon with n sides, the angle of rotation measures $\frac{360°}{n}$. Therefore, a square has rotational symmetry about the angle 90° and its multiples. A regular hexagon has rotational symmetry about the angle 60° and its multiples. A regular octagon has rotational symmetry about 45° and its multiples. And a regular decagon has rotational symmetry about 36° and its multiples. Since 120° is a multiple of 60°, the correct answer is a regular hexagon.

100. C: Since a and b are multiples of 3, each can be expressed as the product of 3 and an integer. So, if we write $a = 3x$ and $b = 3y$, then the equation becomes $4(3x)^2 + (3y)^3 = c$.

$$4(3x)^2 + (3y)^3 = c$$
$$36x^2 + 27y^3 = c$$
$$9(4x^2 + 3y^3) = c$$

Since c is the product of 9 and some other integer, 9 must be a factor of c.

Practice Test #2

1. Milly walks x meters north and $x + 15$ meters east to get to the grocery store. On a neighborhood map which has a scale of 1 cm : 15 m, the distance between Milly's house and the grocery store is 5 cm. How far did Milly walk to the store?

a. 105 m
b. 75 m
c. 60 m
d. 45 m

2. Which of these is the equation of the function graphed below?

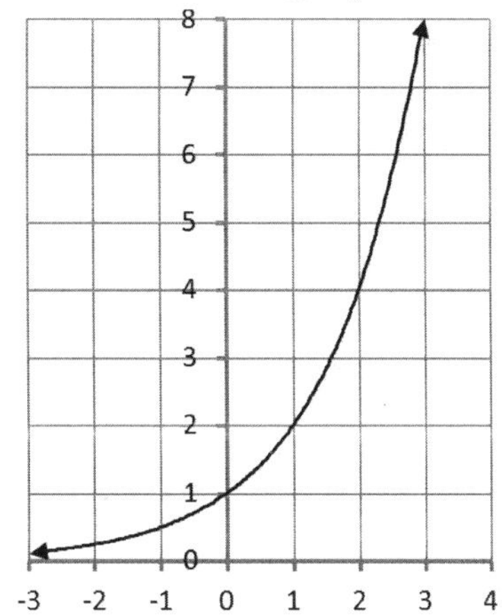

a. $f(x) = x^2$
b. $f(x) = \sqrt{x}$
c. $f(x) = 2^x$
d. $f(x) = \log_2 x$

3. Find $[g \circ f\,]x$ when $f(x) = x + 2$ and $g(x) = 2x^2 - 4x + 2$.

a. $4x^2 + 10x + 6$
b. $2x^2 - 4x + 8$
c. $x^2 - 2$
d. $2x^2 + 4x + 2$

4. What is the radius of the circle defined by the equation $x^2 + y^2 - 4x + 6y - 5 = 0$?

a. $2\sqrt{3}$
b. $3\sqrt{2}$
c. $\sqrt{5}$
d. $2\sqrt{5}$

5. A teacher recorded the dates that students turned in projects in two different classes to compare trends and noticed that a large number of students were submitting their work late. She plotted charts to see how many students in each class were turning in late work and how late they were.

Which of the following is a true statement for these data?

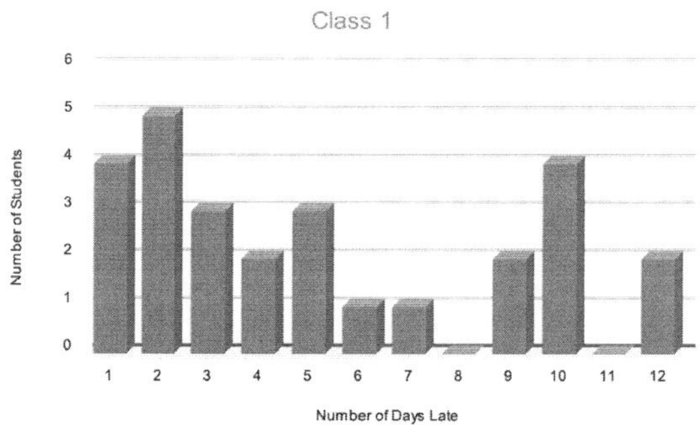

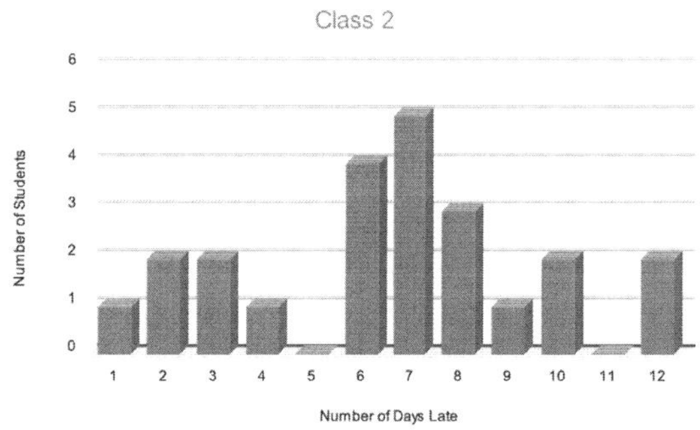

a. The median number of days late in Class 1 is 2 days less than in Class 2.
b. On average, students turned in work 4 days later in Class 2 than in Class 1 (round to nearest whole number).
c. The mode late time is higher for Class 2 than for Class 1.
d. The median late time for Class 1 is greater than the mean for Class 1.

6. Given that x is a whole number greater than 5 and that the greatest common factor of x and y is greater than 1, which of the following must be true?

Quantity A	**Quantity B**
y	the least common multiple of x and y

a. Quantity A $>$ Quantity B
b. Quantity A $<$ Quantity B
c. Quantity A $=$ Quantity B
d. Quantity A $\leq$ Quantity B

7. Aaron goes on a run every morning down the straight country road that he lives on. The graph below shows Aaron's distance from home at times throughout his morning run. Which of the following statements is (are) true?

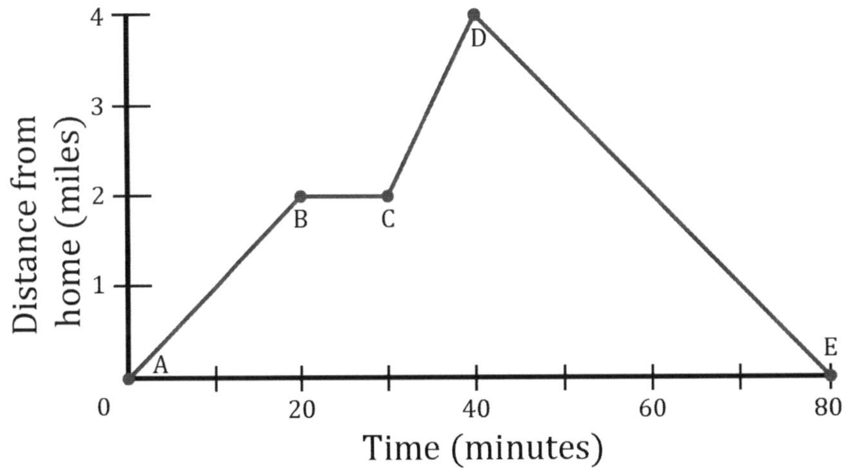

I. Aaron's average running speed was 6 mph.
II. Aaron's running speed from A to B was the same as from D to E.
III. Aaron ran a total distance of four miles.

a. I only
b. II only
c. I and II
d. I, II, and III

8. Which of these represents the equation of a sphere that is centered in the xyz-space at the point $(1, 0, -2)$ and has a volume of 36π cubic units?

a. $x^2 + y^2 + z^2 - 2x + 4z = 4$
b. $x^2 + y^2 + z^2 + 2x - 4z = 4$
c. $x^2 + y^2 + z^2 - 2x + 4z = -2$
d. $x^2 + y^2 + z^2 + 2x - 4z = 2$

9. A teacher sits on the floor with five of her students, seated in a circle. If she must sit next to Andrew, how many distinguishable seating arrangements are there? (If an arrangement is merely a rotation of another arrangement, the two are not distinguishable.)

a. 12
b. 24
c. 48
d. 96

10. If the midpoint of a line segment graphed on the xy-coordinate plane is $(1, -4)$ and the slope of the line segment is 3, which of these is a possible endpoint of the line segment?

a. $(-3, -16)$
b. $(2, -7)$
c. $(-1, 4)$
d. $(5, 9)$

11. A triangle with vertices $A(-4,-3)$, $B(-2,0)$, and $C(-1,-1)$ is reflected across $y = x - 3$ to give $\Delta A'B'C'$, which is subsequently reflected across the y-axis to give $\Delta A''B''C''$. Which of these statements is true?

a. A translation of ΔABC three units up gives $\Delta A''B''C''$.
b. A reflection of ΔABC about the x-axis gives $\Delta A''B''C''$.
c. A 90° rotation of ΔABC about $(0,-3)$ gives $\Delta A''B''C''$.
d. A 270° rotation of ΔABC about $(0,-3)$ gives $\Delta A''B''C''$.

12. When planning a unit on linear equations, a teacher would most likely include discussion on which of the following topics?

a. Conjugating to remove irrational denominators
b. Slope of a straight line
c. Order of operations
d. Characteristics of the diagonals of various quadrilaterals

13. Which of the following is NOT an axiom of Euclidean geometry?

I. Between any two points, a single, straight line segment may be drawn.
II. On any given plane, a circle may be drawn.
III. Any given right angle is congruent to any other right angle.

a. I
b. II
c. I & III
d. I, II, & III

14. If the square of three times the sum of a and six is fourteen more than a, which of these is a possible value of a?

a. $\sqrt{2}$
b. $\frac{3}{2}$
c. 1
d. -5

15. The heights of 200 high school males are normally distributed with a mean height of 67.5 inches and a standard deviation of 3.5 inches. In a normal distribution, approximately 68% of values are within one standard deviation of the mean. About how many individuals from the selected group are shorter than 5'11"?

a. 125
b. 142
c. 168
d. 184

16. To which of the following sets of numbers does $\sqrt{32}$ NOT belong?

I. The set of real numbers
II. The set of rational numbers
III. The set of complex numbers

a. I
b. II only
c. I and III
d. I, II, & III

17. In the following inequality, solve for q.

$$-3q + 12 \geq 4q - 30$$

a. $q \geq 6$
b. $q = 6$
c. $q \neq 6$
d. $q \leq 6$

18. The two prisms shown below are similar (units are inches). What is the measure of x?

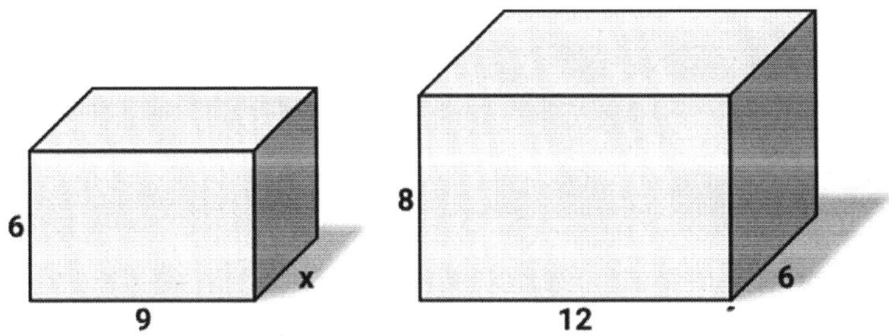

a. $4\frac{1}{2}$ in
b. $4\frac{3}{4}$ in
c. 5 in
d. $5\frac{1}{4}$ in

19. Identical rugs are offered for sale at two local shops and one online retailer, designated Stores A, B, and C, respectively. The rug's regular sales price is $296 at Store A, $220 at Store B, and $198.00 at Store C. Stores A and B collect 8% in sales tax on any after-discount price, while Store C collects no tax but charges a $35 shipping fee. A buyer has a 30% off coupon for Store A and a $10 off coupon for Store B. Which of these lists the stores in order of lowest to highest final sales price after all discounts, taxes, and fees are applied?

a. Store A, Store B, Store C
b. Store B, Store C, Store A
c. Store C, Store A, Store B
d. Store C, Store B, Store A

20. What is thc cxact valuc of tan$\left(\frac{2\pi}{3}\right)$?

a. $-\sqrt{3}$
b. $\frac{\sqrt{3}}{3}$
c. 1

d. $\sqrt{3}$

21. If $2\log_4 y + \log_4 16 = 3$, what is $\log_y 256$?

a. 16
b. 8
c. 4
d. 2

22. A car is driving along the highway at a constant speed when it runs over a pebble, which becomes lodged in one of the tire's treads. If this graph represents the height h of the pebble above the road in inches (y-axis) as a function of time t in seconds (x-axis), which of these statements is true?

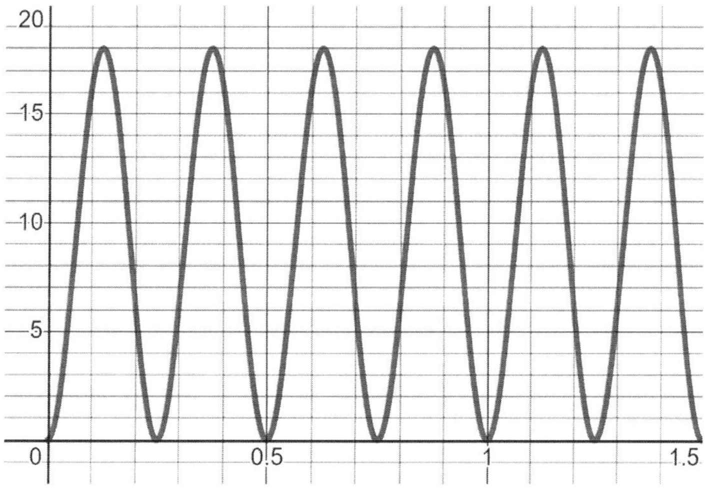

a. The outer radius of the tire is 9 inches, and the tire rotates 240 times per minute.
b. The outer radius of the tire is 18 inches, and the tire rotates 240 times per minute.
c. The outer radius of the tire is 9 inches, and the tire rotates 120 times per minute.
d. The outer radius of the tire is 18 inches, and the tire rotates 120 times per minute.

23. Which of these is a major contribution of the Babylonian civilization to the historical development of mathematics?

a. The division of an hour into 60 minutes, and a minute into 60 seconds, and a circle into 360 degrees
b. The development of algebra as a discipline separate from geometry
c. The use of deductive reasoning in geometric proofs
d. The introduction of Boolean logic

24. Which numeral comes next in the sequence: 54, 59, 63, 68, 72, ...?

a. 76
b. 77
c. 78
d. 79

25. A farmer purchases 32 llamas to raise for their wool. The number of llamas on the farm each year is shown on the table below:

Years after purchase	0	1	2	3
Number of llamas	32	48	72	108

How many llamas should the farmer expect to have 4 years after the original purchase?

a. 144
b. 124
c. 132
d. 162

Refer to the following for questions 26–27:

This data shows the number of students at a high school who are enrolled in various electives.

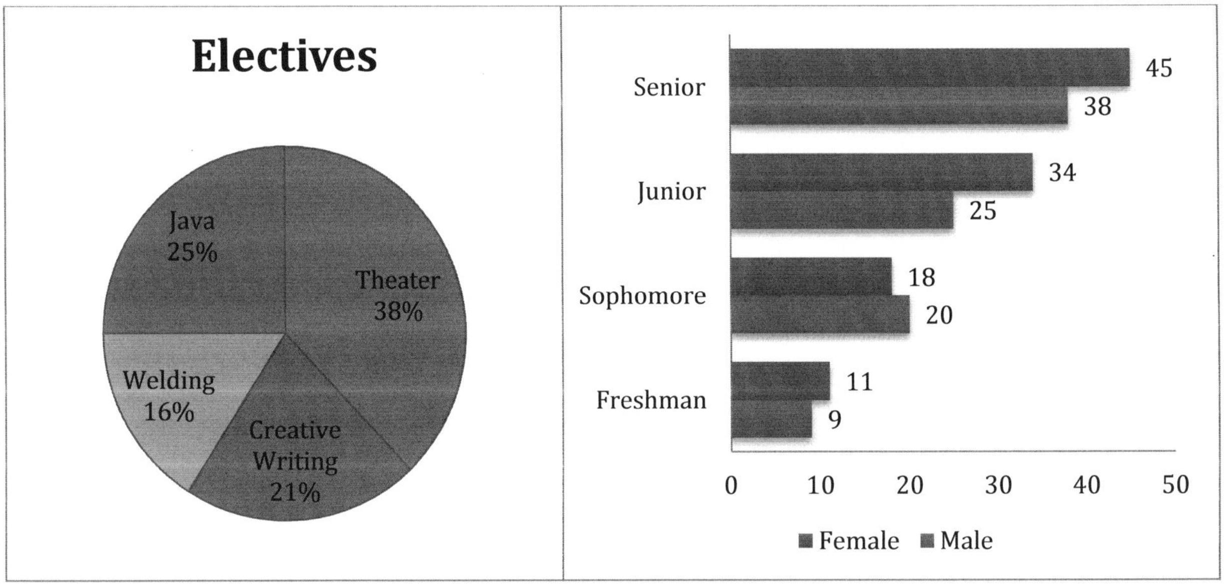

26. A sophomore is randomly selected to be interviewed for the school paper. What is the approximate probability that the student is male?

a. 0.53
b. 0.47
c. 0.19
d. 0.10

27. Which of these is the greatest quantity?

a. The number of students taking welding
b. The number of male sophomores taking an elective
c. The difference in the number of male and female students taking an elective
d. The difference in the number of juniors and seniors taking an elective

28. For ΔABC, what is the length of $\overline{BC}$?

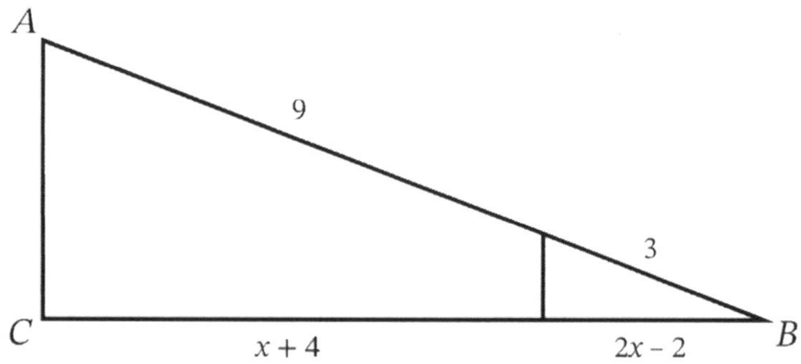

a. 2
b. 6
c. 8
d. 9

Refer to the following for question 29:

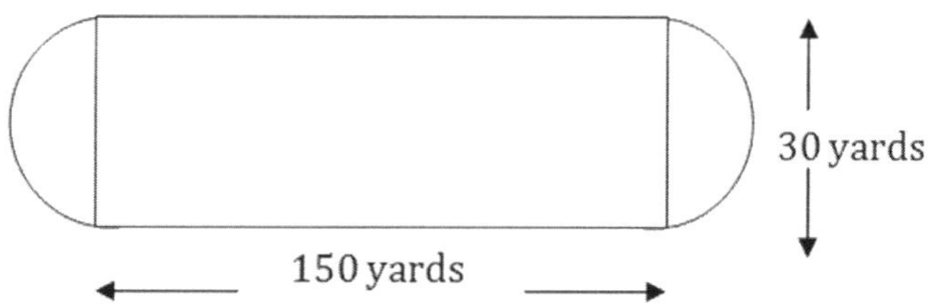

29. A company is building a track for a local high school. There are two straight sections and two semi-circular turns. Given the dimensions, which of the following most closely measures the perimeter of the entire track?

a. 180 yards
b. 300 yards
c. 360 yards
d. 395 yards

30. A round table has six chairs, labeled H–M. If the chairs were arranged in a straight line in the same order that they have around the table, chair H would be on one end and chair K on the other. Chair J would be between chairs H and I, chair L would be between chairs I and M, and chair M would be between chairs L and K. Which of the statements is/are necessarily true based solely on the information provided?

I. The distance between chairs H and L is greater than the distance between chairs I and M.
II. Chair I is between chairs J and L.
III. The distance between chairs M and K is less than the distance between chairs H and L.

a. I, II, and III
b. I and III
c. II only
d. None of these is necessarily true

31. The graph of $f(x)$ is a parabola with a focus of $(a, 3)$ and a directrix of $y = -1$, and $g(x)$ represents a transformation of $f(x)$. If the vertex of the graph of $g(x)$ is $(a, 1)$, which of these is a possible equation for $g(x)$ for nonzero integers a and b?

a. $g(x) = f(x) + 3$
b. $g(x) = 2f(x)$
c. $g(x) = f(x + a)$
d. $g(x) = f(x - a) + 3$

32. An adjunct professor teaches three classes. The number of women and men in each class are shown below. Two individuals are chosen at random to attend a conference with the professor. What is the approximate probability that two men from the same class will be chosen?

	Class 1	Class 2	Class 3
Women	9	21	17
Men	13	14	19

a. 7.9%
b. 9.6%
c. 11.9%
d. 13.8%

33. A 6th grade math teacher is introducing the concept of positive and negative numbers to a group of students. Which of the following models would be the most effective when introducing this concept?

a. Fraction strips
b. Venn diagrams
c. Shaded regions
d. Number lines

34. A random sample of 250 students at a high school were asked these three questions:

Do you drink coffee?
Do you drink tea?
Do you drink hot chocolate?

The results of the survey are shown below. If these data are representative of the population of students at the school, which of these is most probable?

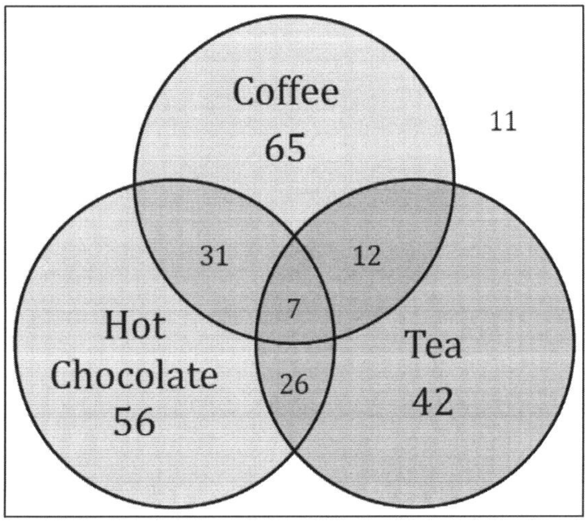

a. A student chosen at random drinks tea.
b. If a student chosen at random drinks hot chocolate, he also drinks at least one other beverage.
c. If a student chosen at random drinks coffee and hot chocolate, he also drinks tea.
d. A student chosen at random does not drink coffee, tea, or hot chocolate.

35. In reviewing her lesson plans and test data following the completion of a unit, which of the following should the teacher be most concerned about regarding her students?

a. Multiple students finished the project two days before it was due, and she had to quickly create enrichment activities for them to complete so they would not become bored and distract others
b. Two lessons took longer than anticipated due to student questioning and classroom engagement
c. Several students with documented learning disabilities struggled with the unit and were unable to complete their project
d. ELL students had to use their translators and dictionaries on difficult vocabulary more than they have in the past

36. As shown below, six congruent isosceles trapezoids are fitted together. Find the value of the angle x.

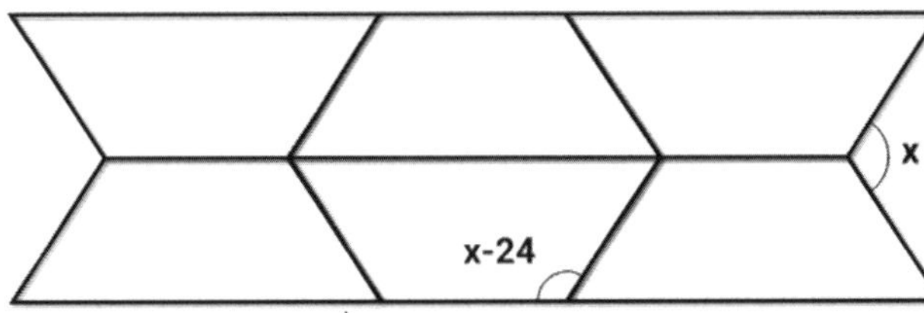

a. $x = 92°$
b. $x = 104°$
c. $x = 136°$
d. $x = 125°$

37. Katrina wants to solve this math problem: "If there are 30 days in a month and today is the 12th, how many days until the end of the month?" What should be her first problem-solving step?

a. Devise a plan for solving the problem
b. Carry out the plan she created
c. Look back to check that her answer is correct
d. Understand what the problem is asking

38. Which of these would best illustrate the percentage of a budget allocated to various departments?

a. Pie chart
b. Line graph
c. Box-and-whisker plot
d. Venn diagram

39. Ms. Robinson has a busy afternoon delivering gifts to family members. First, she drives 5.1 miles to her mother's house. Then, she drives 7.2 miles to her aunt's house, followed by 13.9 miles to her brother's house. Finally, she drives 14.6 miles on the return trip home. What is the best estimate of the total miles Ms. Robinson drives on her trip?

a. 29 miles
b. 41 miles
c. 39 miles
d. 42 miles

40. To test the accuracy and precision of two scales, a student repeatedly measured the mass of a 10g standard and recorded these results.

	Trial 1	Trial 2	Trial 3	Trial 4
Scale 1	9.99 g	9.98 g	10.02g	10.01g
Scale 2	10.206 g	10.209 g	10.210 g	10.208 g

Which of these conclusions about the scales is true?

a. Scale 1 has an average percent error of 0.15%, and Scale 2 has an average percent error of 2.08%. Scale 1 is more accurate and precise than Scale 2.
b. Scale 1 has an average percent error of 0.15%, and Scale 2 has an average percent error of 2.08%. Scale 1 is more accurate than Scale 2; however, Scale 2 is more precise.
c. Scale 1 has an average percent error of 0%, and Scale 2 has an average percent error of 2.08%. Scale 1 is more accurate and precise than Scale 2.
d. Scale 1 has an average percent error of 0%, and Scale 2 has an average percent error of 2.08%. Scale 1 is more accurate than Scale 2; however, Scale 2 is more precise.

41. Solve $4x^3y^2 - 16x^2y = -16x^3y + 4x^2y^2$ for x.

a. $x = \{0\}$
b. $x = \{0,1\}$
c. $x = \{-4\}$
d. $x = \{-4,0,1\}$

42. Alex is working through some multiplication problems on his homework. He solves both problems incorrectly, as illustrated below. If he makes the same mistake using the same strategy to solve 174×2, what will his answer be?

#1	#2
$\begin{array}{r} 143 \\ \times\ 3 \\ \hline 3{,}129 \end{array}$	$\begin{array}{r} 214 \\ \times\ 4 \\ \hline 8{,}416 \end{array}$

a. 429
b. 349
c. 1,209
d. 2,148

43. Simplify: $(4 - i)^2 - (2 - 4i)$.

a. $\sqrt{185}$
b. $13 - 4i$
c. $13 + 4i$
d. 17

44. Express the area of the given right triangle as a function of x.

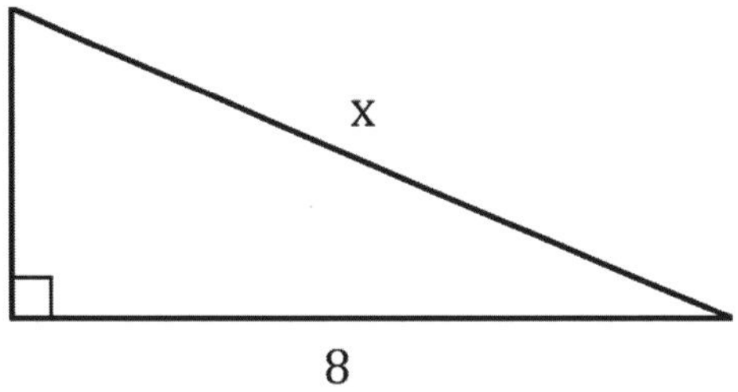

a. $A(x) = 4x$
b. $A(x) = \frac{x\sqrt{64-x^2}}{2}$
c. $A(x) = 4\sqrt{x^2 - 64}$
d. $A(x) = 64 - \sqrt{x^2}$

45. On a floor plan drawn at a scale of 1 : 100, the area of a rectangular room is 30 cm^2. What is the actual area of the room?

a. 30,000 cm^2
b. 300 m^2
c. 3,000 m^2
d. 30 m^2

Refer to the following for question 46:

Consider the following graphic showing demographics of a high school with 1,219 total students:

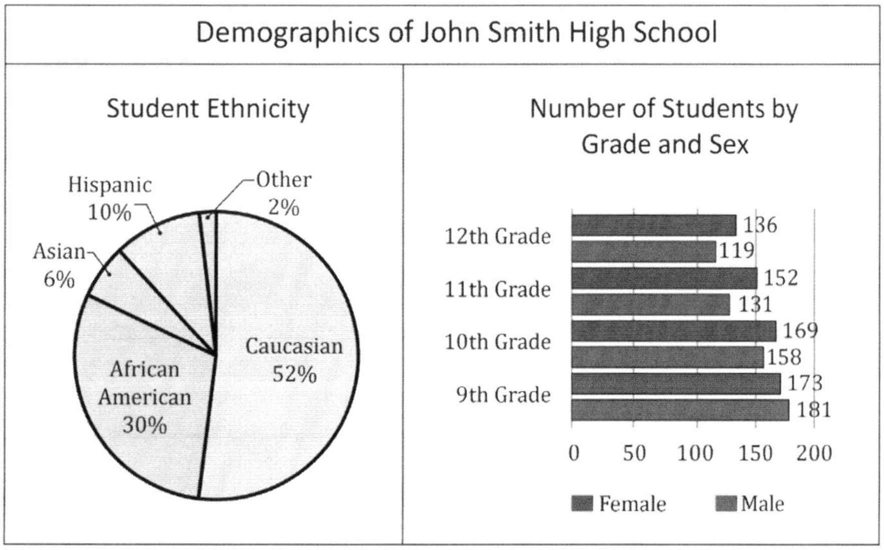

46. An eleventh grader is chosen at random to represent the school at a conference. What is the approximate probability that the student is male?

a. 0.03
b. 0.11
c. 0.22
d. 0.46

47. Which of these describes the graph of the equation $2x^2 - 3y^2 - 12x + 6y - 15 = 0$?

a. Circular
b. Elliptical
c. Parabolic
d. Hyperbolic

48. Mr. Foster wants to put new carpet on the floor of his rectangular playroom. The playroom is 27 feet long and 18 feet wide. He has found an inexpensive carpet that is priced $14 per square yard. What would be a reasonable price for enough carpet to cover the floor of his playroom?

a. $486
b. $756
c. $1,260
d. $2,268

49. Which of these tables properly displays the measures of central tendency that can be used for nominal, interval, and ordinal data?

a.

	Mean	Median	Mode
Nominal			x
Interval	x	x	x
Ordinal		x	x

b.

	Mean	Median	Mode
Nominal			x
Interval	x	x	x
Ordinal	x	x	x

c.

	Mean	Median	Mode
Nominal	x	x	x
Interval	x	x	x
Ordinal	x	x	x

d.

	Mean	Median	Mode
Nominal			x
Interval	x	x	
Ordinal	x	x	x

50. Line segment $\overline{PQ}$ has endpoints (a, b) and (c, b). If $\overline{P'Q'}$ is the translation of $\overline{PQ}$ along a diagonal line such that P' is located at point (c, d), what is the area of quadrilateral $PP'Q'Q$?

a. $|a - c| \times |b - d|$
b. $|a - b| \times |c - d|$
c. $|a - d| \times |b - c|$
d. $(a - c)^2$

51. Calculate: $\int 3x^2 e^{x^3}\,dx$

a. $x^3 e^{x^3} + C$
b. $e^{x^3} + C$
c. $x^3 e^{\frac{x^4}{4}} + C$
d. $\ln x^3 + C$

52. Bruce is attending a conference that is 827 km from his home. If he travels at a speed of 64 km/hour, approximately how long will it take him to reach his destination?

a. 5 hours
b. 9 hours
c. 13 hours
d. 17 hours

53. Which of these relationships represents y as a function of x?

a. $x^2 + y^2 = 16$

b. 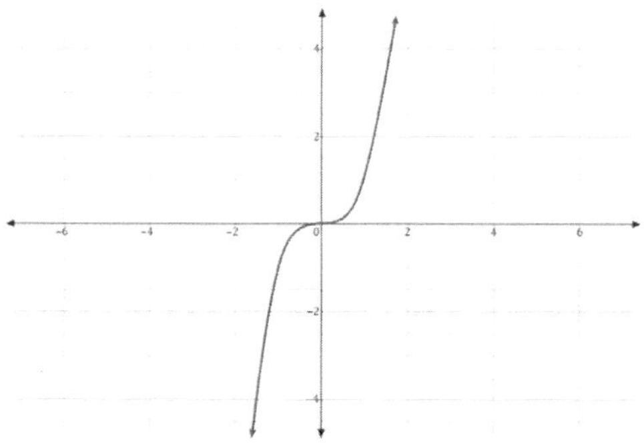

c. $y = \pm\sqrt{x}$

d. 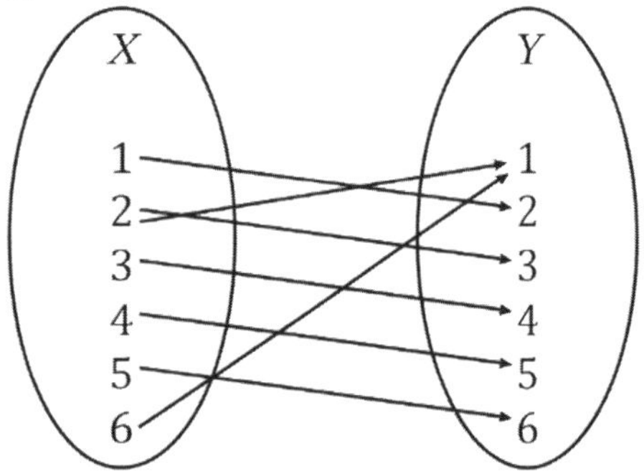

54. Ms. Byrne stresses the importance of daily math homework with her sixth- and seventh-grade students. She states that the consistent practice will help students solidify their understanding of mathematical principles. Ms. Byrne also reviews this homework on a daily basis to help her understand what the students understand and to guide her instruction. This practice is an example of:

a. Summative assessment
b. Diversity in assignments
c. Formative assessment
d. Standards set forth for middle-grade mathematics

55. In ΔABC, if $\sin A = \cos 62°$, what is $\cos A$?

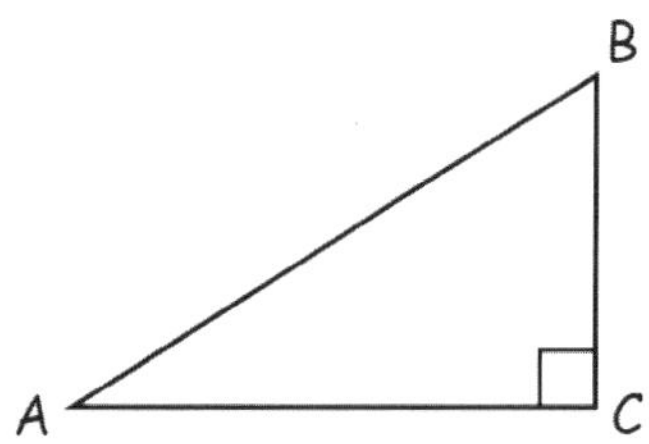

a. $\sin 28°$
b. $\sin 62°$
c. $\cos 62°$
d. $\sec 28°$

56. In order to analyze the real estate market for two different zip codes within the city, a realtor examined the most recent 100 home sales in each zip code. She considered a house which sold within the first month of its listing to have a market time of one month; likewise, she considered a house to have a market time of two months if it sold after having been on the market for more than one month but before the end of the second month. Using this definition of market time, she determined the frequency of sales by the number of months on the market. The results are displayed below. Which of the following is a true statement for these data?

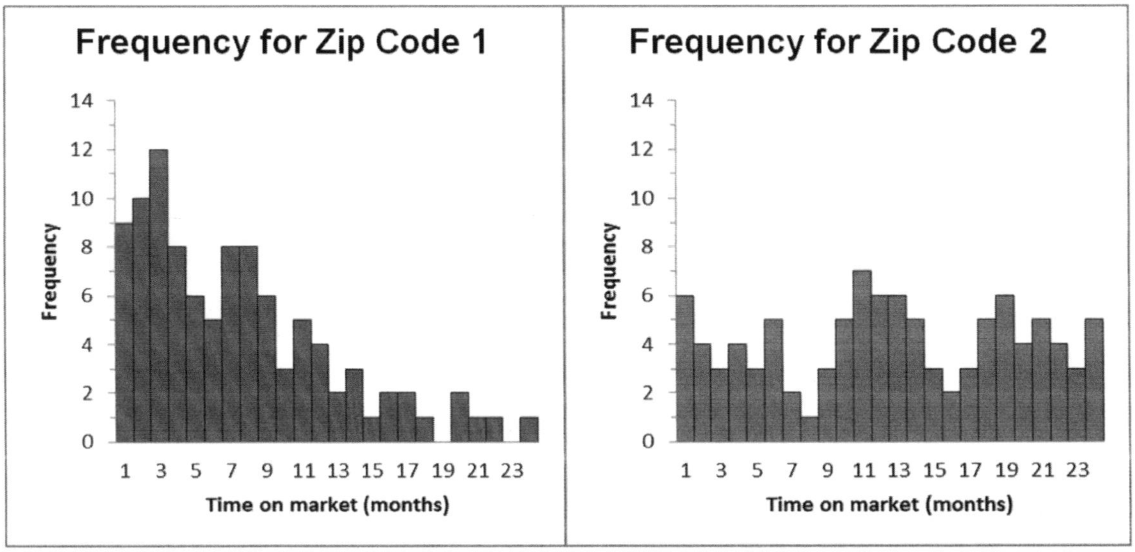

a. The median time a house spent on the market in Zip Code 1 is five months less than Zip Code 2.
b. On average, a house spent seven months longer on the market in Zip Code 2 than in Zip Code 1.
c. The mode time on the market is higher for Zip Code 1 than for Zip Code 2.
d. The median time on the market is less than the mean time on the market for Zip Code 1.

57. A colony of Escherichia coli is inoculated from a Petri dish into a test tube containing 50 mL of nutrient broth. The test tube is placed in a 37 °C incubator and agitator. After one hour, the number of bacteria in the test tube is determined to be 8×10^6. Given that the doubling time of Escherichia coli is 20 minutes with agitation at 37 °C, approximately how many bacteria should the test tube contain after eight hours of growth?

a. 2.56×10^8
b. 2.05×10^9
c. 1.7×10^{14}
d. 1.7×10^{13}

58. Which of these defines the recursive sequence $a_1 = -2, a_{n+1} = a_n + \frac{1}{2}$ explicitly?

a. $a_n = \frac{1}{2}n - 2$
b. $a_n = -2n + \frac{1}{2}$
c. $a_n = \frac{1}{2}n - \frac{5}{2}$
d. $a_n = -2n + \frac{5}{2}$

59. The game commission releases 16 wolves into a state park. The number of wolves over the next several years is shown on the table below:

Years after release	0	1	2	3
Number of wolves	16	24	36	54

How many wolves should the game commission expect to find 4 years after the release of the original 16 wolves?

a. 72
b. 81
c. 66
d. 62

60. What is the converse of the statement below?

If I see a robin, it is spring.

a. If it is not spring, I do not see a robin.
b. If it is spring, I do not see a robin.
c. If I do not see a robin, it is not spring.
d. If it is spring, I see a robin.

61. Simplify:

$$\begin{bmatrix} 2 & 0 & -5 \end{bmatrix}\left(\begin{bmatrix} 4 \\ 2 \\ -1 \end{bmatrix} - \begin{bmatrix} 3 \\ 5 \\ -5 \end{bmatrix}\right)$$

a. $\begin{bmatrix} -18 \end{bmatrix}$
b. $\begin{bmatrix} 2 \\ 0 \\ -20 \end{bmatrix}$
c. $\begin{bmatrix} 2 & 0 & -20 \end{bmatrix}$
d. $\begin{bmatrix} 2 & 0 & -5 \\ -6 & 0 & 15 \\ 8 & 0 & -20 \end{bmatrix}$

62. To which of the following sets of numbers does –4 NOT belong?

a. The set of whole numbers
b. The set of rational numbers
c. The set of integers
d. The set of real numbers

63. A homeowner is ordering fencing material to place a fence around her property. The lot is rectangular with a length of 385 feet, and the width is 295 feet. Which of the following is the best estimate of the minimum amount of fencing material she should order?

a. 1600 feet
b. 700 feet
c. 1,400 feet
d. 1,200 feet

Refer to the following for questions 64–65:

The diagrams below show the number of people in a small town who participate in various types of volunteer work.

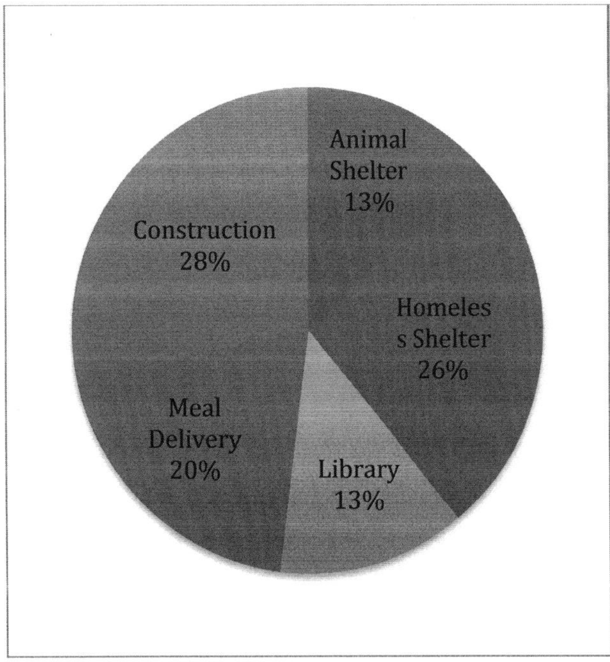

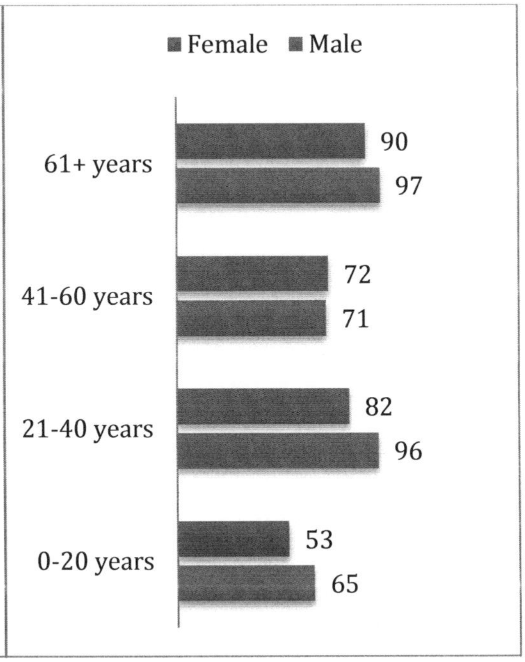

64. Which of these is the greatest quantity?

a. The average number of females per age bracket
b. The number of volunteers at the animal shelter
c. The difference in the number of male and female volunteers
d. The difference in the number of volunteers over age 60 and under age 21

65. A volunteer under age 21 is chosen at random for a scholarship. What is the approximate probability that the student is male?

a. 0.47
b. 0.51
c. 0.55
d. 0.58

66. Of the following, which is/are NOT an example(s) of math manipulatives?

a. Tangrams for shape recognition
b. Large magnetic number boards
c. Printed mathematical formulas
d. Play money and toy cash registers

67. Which of these equations is represented by the graph below?

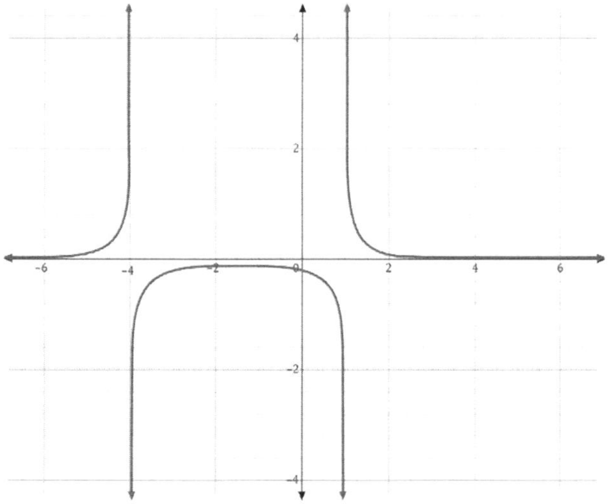

a. $y = \frac{2x-2}{x^2+3x-4}$
b. $y = \frac{1}{x^2+3x-4}$
c. $y = \frac{1}{x+4} + \frac{1}{x-1}$
d. $y = \frac{x}{x^2+3x-4}$

68. Which of these is true about having an awareness of patterns and relationships in the real world?

a. It does not inform our understanding of the basic structure of things.
b. It helps us understand series of events, but not predict future ones.
c. It is unrelated to our basic feeling of confidence in the environment.
d. It increases our self-efficacy about interacting with our environment.

69. Which of these does NOT simulate randomly selecting a person from a group of 11?

a. Assigning each student a unique card value of A, 2, 3, 4, 5, 6, 7, 8, 9, 10, or J and drawing a single card from a deck of cards, redrawing if an invalid card is selected.
b. Assigning each student a unique number 2–12 and rolling a pair of dice to determine which student is selected.
c. Assigning each student a unique letter A–K, labeling 11 index cards A–K, and blindly drawing one.
d. Assigning each student a unique numeric value of 1–11 and spinning a spinner mounted on a 11-section wheel.

70. In addition to math, in which other area of life do we tend to see patterns and relationships?

a. Works of art
b. Pieces of music
c. Articles of clothing
d. In all of these areas

71. If $\sin\theta = \frac{1}{2}$ when $\frac{\pi}{2} < \theta < \pi$, what is the value of θ?

a. $\frac{\pi}{6}$
b. $\frac{\pi}{3}$
c. $\frac{2\pi}{3}$
d. $\frac{5\pi}{6}$

72. What is the most accurate indicator of overall student performance?

a. Final exams and other tests that cover course material on a comprehensive basis.
b. The combined results of frequent evaluations given throughout the term.
c. Studies show that in the end, a teacher's gut instinct about at student is usually right.
d. Homework and papers are usually the best indicator, since they show how a student thinks when not under direct teacher supervision.

73. Solve the system of equations: $\begin{cases} -4x + 3y = 8 \\ 6x - 2y = -7 \end{cases}$

a. $\left(\frac{1}{2}, \frac{10}{3}\right)$
b. $\left(-1, \frac{3}{2}\right)$
c. $\left(2, -\frac{5}{2}\right)$
d. $\left(-\frac{1}{2}, 2\right)$

74. Which of the following piecewise functions can describe the graph below?

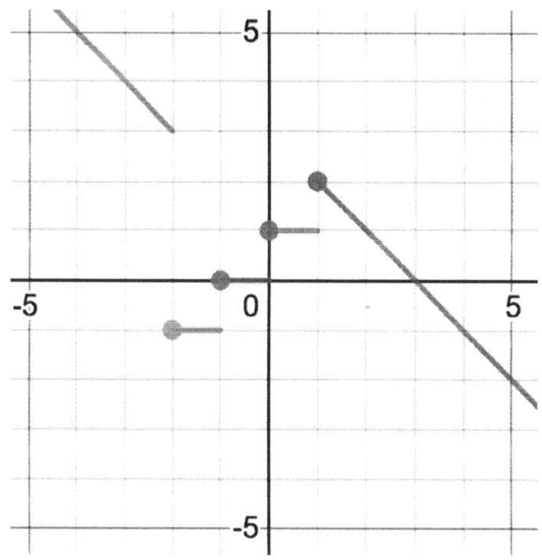

a. $f(x) = \begin{cases} -x + 1 & x < -2 \\ [\![x]\!] & -2 \le x < 1 \\ -2x + 3 & x \ge 1 \end{cases}$

b. $f(x) = \begin{cases} -x + 1 & x \le -2 \\ [\![x + 1]\!] & -2 \le x < 1 \\ -x + 3 & x \ge 1 \end{cases}$

c. $f(x) = \begin{cases} -x + 1 & x < -2 \\ [\![x]\!] + 1 & -2 \le x < 1 \\ -x + 3 & x \ge 2 \end{cases}$

d. $f(x) = \begin{cases} -x + 1 & x \le -2 \\ [\![x - 1]\!] & -2 < x \le 1 \\ -2x + 6 & x > 1 \end{cases}$

75. Which number comes next in the sequence: 1, 4, 9, 16, ...?

a. 20
b. 24
c. 25
d. 32

76. Which of these statements is NOT necessarily true when $f(x) = \log_b x$ and $b > 1$?

a. The x-intercept of the graph of $f(x)$ is $(1, 0)$.
b. The graph of $f(x)$ passes through $(b, 1)$.
c. $f(x) < 0$ when $0 < x < 1$.
d. If $g(x) = x^b$, the graph of $f(x)$ is symmetric to the graph of $g(x)$ with respect to $y = x$.

77. Solve $\frac{x-2}{x-1} = \frac{x-1}{x+1} + \frac{2}{x-1}$.

a. $x = 2$
b. $x = -5$
c. $x = 1$
d. No solution

78. Zeke drove from his house to a furniture store in Atlanta and then back home along the same route. It took Zeke three hours to drive to the store. By driving an average of 20 mph faster on his return trip, Zeke was able to save an hour of driving time. What was Zeke's average driving speed on his round trip?

a. 24 mph
b. 48 mph
c. 50 mph
d. 60 mph

79. Mr. Aguilera needs 71 feet of fencing that costs $3.98 per foot. Which of the following is the best approximation for the price of the fencing?

a. $210
b. $240
c. $280
d. $320

80. Given that x is a prime number and the greatest common factor of x and y is greater than 1, compare the two quantities.

Quantity A	Quantity B
y	the least common multiple of x and y

a. Quantity A is greater.
b. Quantity B is greater.
c. The two quantities are the same.
d. The relationship cannot be determined from the given information.

81. What is the sum of the series $200 + 100 + 50 + 25 + \cdots$?

a. 375
b. 400
c. 600
d. The sum is infinite.

82. The cost, in dollars, of shipping x computers to California for sale is $3,000 + 100x$. The amount received when selling these computers is $400x$ dollars. What is the least number of computers that must be shipped and sold so that the amount received is at least equal to the shipping cost?

a. 10 computers
b. 15 computers
c. 20 computers
d. 25 computers
e. 30 computers

83. A teacher wishes to divide her class of 20 students into 4 groups, each of which will have 3 boys and 2 girls. How many different ways are there to form a single group?

a. 248
b. 6,160
c. 73,920
d. 95,040

84. Given the function $f(x) = 10^x$. If $f(x) = 1$, which of these approximates x?

a. 0.1
b. 0
c. 1
d. 10

85. Ride Service A charges a flat rate of \$10 for the first 10 miles, plus 25 cents per mile for anything over 10 miles. Ride Service B charges 40 cents per mile. Both services charge the same for a trip that is how long?

a. 40 miles
b. 45 miles
c. 50 miles
d. 55 miles

86. Natasha designs a square pyramidal tent for her children. Each of the sides of the square base measures x ft, and the tent's height is h feet. If Natasha were to increase by 1 ft the length of each side of the base, how much more interior space would the tent have?

a. $\frac{x^2h+2xh+h}{3}$ ft^3
b. $\frac{2xh+h}{3}$ ft^3
c. $\frac{x^2h+3}{3}$ ft^3
d. 1 ft^3

87. Which of the following statements is (are) true when $f(x) = \frac{x^2-2x-3}{x^3+3x^2-6x-8}$?

I. The graph $f(x)$ has two vertical asymptotes at $x = 2$ and $x = -4$.
II. The x- and y-intercepts of the graph of $f(x)$ are both 3.

a. I
b. II
c. I and II
d. Neither statement is true.

88. If $\cos\theta + 1 = 0$, which of the following is a possible value of θ?

a. -180°
b. -90°
c. 0°
d. 135°

89. Which of the following could be the graph of $y = -a(x+b)(x+c)^2$ if $a > 0$?

a.

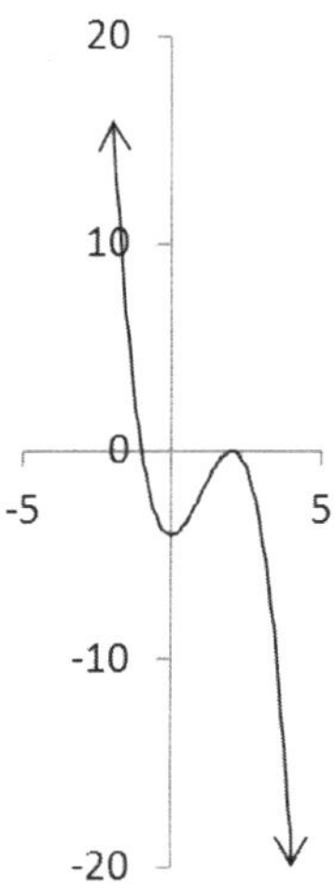

b.

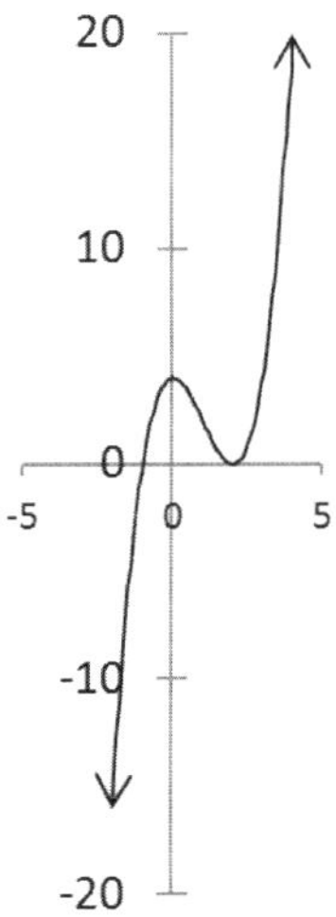

c.

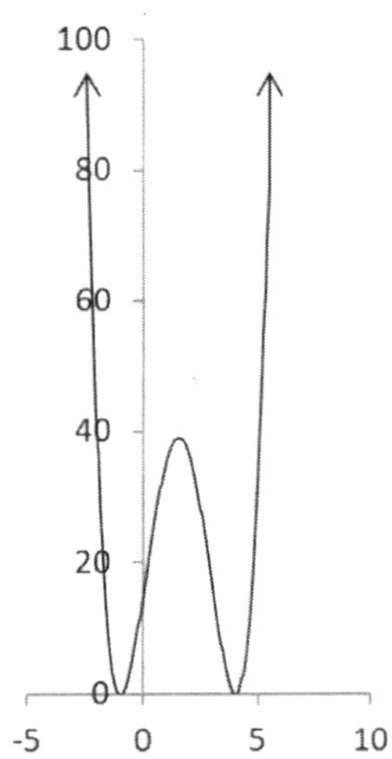

d.

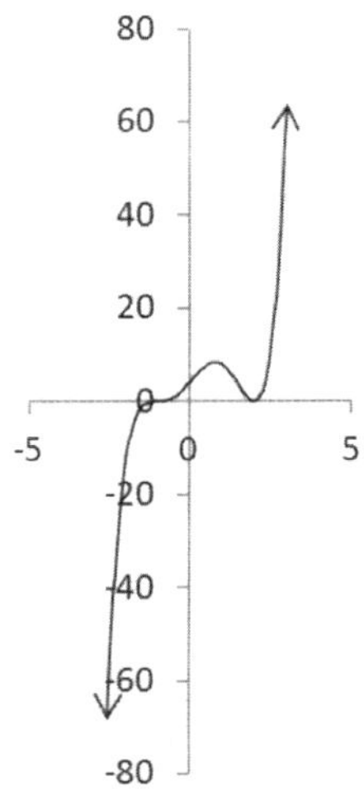

90. Which of the following statements is (are) true when $f(x) = \frac{x^2-x-6}{x^3+2x^2-x-2}$?

I. The graph $f(x)$ has vertical asymptotes at $x = -2$, $x = -1$, and $x = 1$.
II. The x- and y-intercepts of the graph of $f(x)$ are both 3.

a. I only
b. II only
c. I and II
d. Neither statement is true.

91. Which of these is NOT a net of a cube?

a. b. c. d.

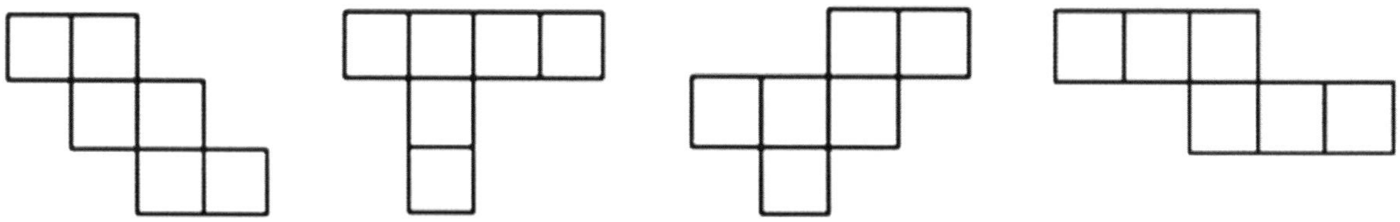

92. A man looks out of a window of a tall building at a 45° angle of depression and sees his car in the parking lot. When he turns his gaze downward to a 60° angle of depression, he sees his wife's car. If his car is parked 60 feet from his wife's car, about how far from the building did his wife park her car?

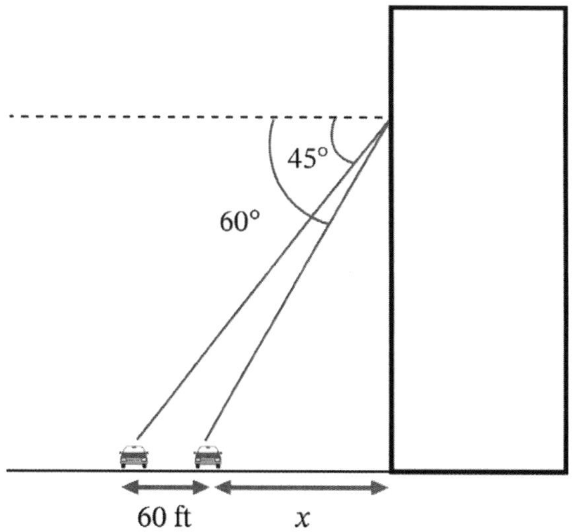

a. 163 feet
b. 122 feet
c. 82 feet
d. 60 feet

93. Solve $5x^2 - 4x = -2$.

a. $x = \frac{2 \pm \sqrt{14}i}{5}$
b. $x = \pm i\sqrt{24}$
c. $x = \pm\frac{2\sqrt{2}i}{5}$
d. $x = \frac{2 \pm i\sqrt{6}}{5}$

94. Simplify the expression $\sqrt{\frac{-54x^5}{80y^6}}$.

a. $\frac{3x^2 i\sqrt{6x}}{20y^3}$
b. $\frac{3x^2 i\sqrt{6x}}{4y^3}$
c. $\frac{-3x^2 i\sqrt{30x}}{8y^3}$
d. $\frac{3x^2 i\sqrt{30x}}{20y^3}$

95. Tessa rode her bike to the lake in an hour and 15 minutes. On her way home, she rode 4 mph faster and arrived in 45 minutes. What was her average speed on her round trip?

a. 3.5 mph
b. 5.5 mph
c. 7.5 mph
d. 9.5 mph

96. Which of the following expressions is equal to $\sin\theta \sec\theta$?

a. $\cot\theta$
b. $\tan\theta$
c. $\csc\theta$
d. $\sec\theta - 1$

97. A circle is inscribed inside quadrilateral $ABCD$. $\overline{CD}$ is bisected by the point at which it is tangent to the circle. If $\overline{AB} = 14$, $\overline{BC} = 10$, $\overline{CD} = 8$, then which of the following statements is true?

a. $\overline{AD} = 11$
b. $\overline{AD} = 2\sqrt{34}$
c. $\overline{AD} = 12$
d. $\overline{AD} = 17.5$

98. Which of these statements is (are) true for the function $g(x)$?

$$g(x) = \begin{cases} -x + 3 & x < 2 \\ 2x - 1 & x \geq 2 \end{cases}$$

I. $g(3) = 0$
II. The graph of $g(x)$ is discontinuous at $x = 2$.
III. The range of $g(x)$ is all real numbers.

a. II only
b. III only
c. I and II
d. II and III

99. Which of the graphs below represents $f(x) = -3|-x + 2| +$?

a. 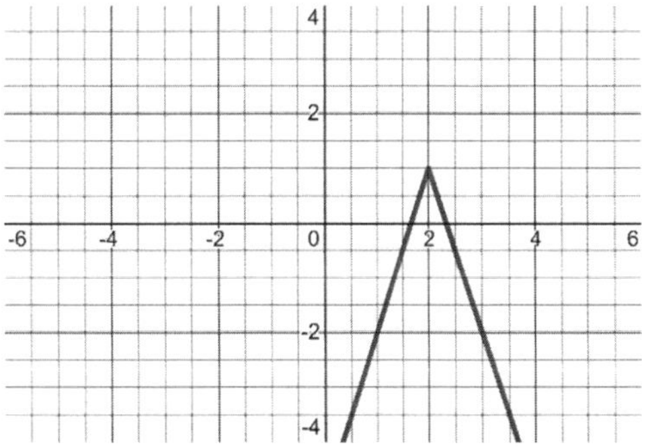

c. 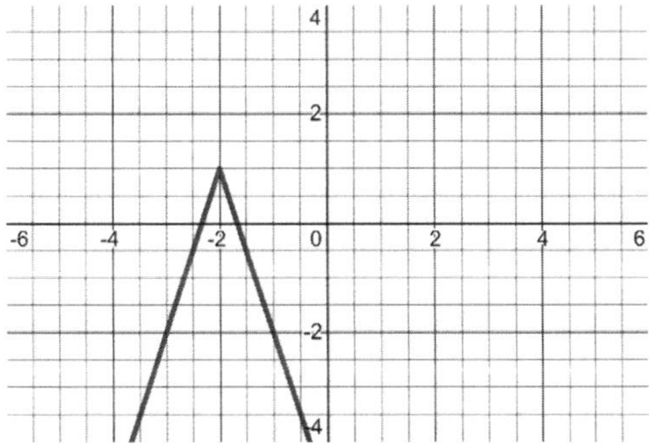

b. 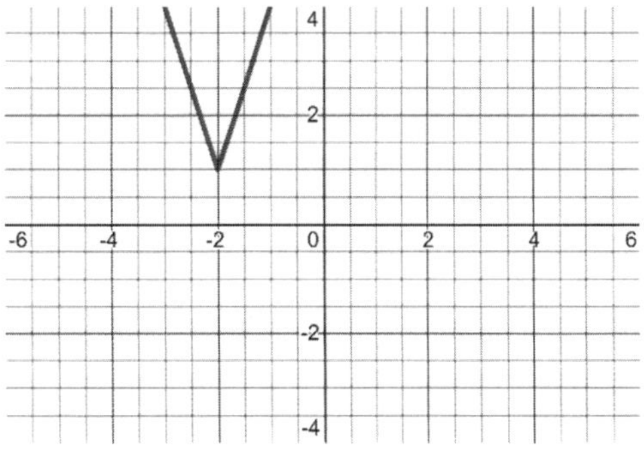

d. 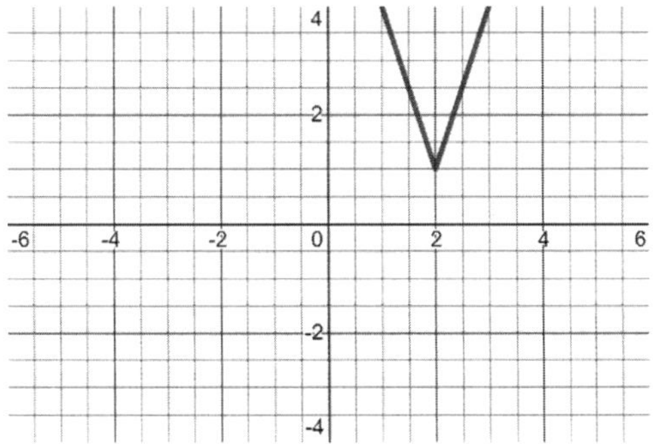

100. Which mathematician is responsible for what is often called the most remarkable and beautiful mathematical formula, $e^{i\pi} + 1 = 0$?

a. Pythagoras
b. Euclid
c. Euler
d. Fermat

Answer Key and Explanations for Test #2

1. A: If the distance is 5 cm on the map, then the actual distance is $5 \times 15 = 75$ m. To find x, use the Pythagorean theorem.

$$x^2 + (x + 15)^2 = (75)^2$$
$$x^2 + x^2 + 30x + 225 = 5{,}625$$
$$2x^2 + 30x - 5{,}400 = 0$$
$$2(x^2 + 15x - 2{,}700) = 0$$
$$2(x - 45)(x + 60) = 0$$
$$x = 45 \quad x = -60$$

Since x represents a distance in this situation, use the positive value. Since $x = 45$, $x + 15 = 60$. Milly walks a total of $45 + 60 = 105$ m to get to the store.

2. C: The graph shown is the exponential function $y = 2^x$. Notice that the graph passes through (0,1) and (2,4). A quick check of each option can be done to eliminate answer choices.

x	x^2	$\sqrt{x}$	2^x	$\log_2 x$
0	0	0	1	undefined
2	4	$\sqrt{2}$	4	1

3. D: Substitute $x + 2$ for x in the function $g(x)$ and simplify.

$$\begin{aligned}[g \circ f\,]x &= g(f(x)) \\ &= g(x + 2) \\ &= 2(x + 2)^2 - 4(x + 2) + 2 \\ &= 2(x^2 + 4x + 4) - 4(x + 2) + 2 \\ &= 2x^2 + 8x + 8 - 4x - 8 + 2 \\ &= 2x^2 + 4x + 2\end{aligned}$$

4. B: The equation of the circle is given in general form. When the equation is written in the standard form $(x - h)^2 + (y - k)^2 = r^2$, where (h, k) is the center of the circle and r is the radius of the circle, the radius is easy to determine. Putting the equation into standard form requires completing the square for x and y.

$$x^2 + y^2 - 4x + 6y = 5$$
$$(x^2 - 4x + 4) + (y^2 + 6y + 9) = 5 + 4 + 9$$
$$(x - 2)^2 + (y + 3)^2 = 18$$

Since $r^2 = 18$, and since r must be a positive number, $r = \sqrt{18} = 3\sqrt{2}$.

5. C: In Class 1, 27 students submitted late work, so the median is between the 13th and 14th piece of homework. Both the 13th and 14th fall on Day 4, so the median for Class 1 is 4. In Class 2, 23 students submitted late work, so the median is at the 12th piece of homework. This falls on Day 7. So, because $7 - 4 = 3$, the median number of days late in Class 1 is 3 less than the median number of days late in Class 2.

To find the mean late time for each class, find the sum of the late times and divide by the number of students turning in late work in each class. If the frequency of a one-day late time is 4, the number 1 is added four times (1×4), if frequency of a two-day late time is 5, the number 2 is added five times (2×5), and so on. So, to find the average turn-in time, divide the sum of the products of each late time and its corresponding frequency by the number of late turn-ins in each class. For Class 1, the mean late time is 5.22 days, which rounds to approximately 5 days.

$$\text{Mean} = \frac{4(1) + 5(2) + 3(3) + 2(4) + 3(5) + 1(6) + 1(7) + 2(9) + 4(10) + 2(12)}{4 + 5 + 3 + 2 + 3 + 1 + 1 + 2 + 4 + 2} = \frac{141}{27} \approx 5.22$$

For Class 2, the mean late time is 6.57, which rounds to approximately 7 days.

$$\text{Mean} = \frac{1(1) + 2(2) + 2(3) + 1(4) + 4(6) + 5(7) + 3(8) + 1(9) + 2(10) + 2(12)}{1 + 2 + 2 + 1 + 4 + 5 + 3 + 1 + 2 + 2} = \frac{151}{23} \approx 6.57$$

So, because $7 - 5 = 2$, the students in Class 2 turned in work 2 days later than in Class 1.

The mode late time is the date for which the frequency is the highest. For Class 1, the mode late time is 2 days, and for Class 2, the mode late time is 7 days.

The median late time for Class 1 is 4 and the mean is 4.96, so the median late time is less than the mean.

6. D: If x is a whole number greater than 5 and the greatest common factor of x and y is greater than 1, the greatest common factor of x and y must be at least as great as y. For example, if x is 6 and y is 12, the greatest common factor is 6 and the least common multiple is 12, which is equal to y. Or if x is 6 and y is 10, the greatest common factor is 2 and the least common multiple is 30, which is greater than y. If x is 6 and y is 6, then the greatest common factor and least common multiple are both 6, making the quantities equal.

7. C: Aaron ran four miles from home and then back again, so he ran a total of eight miles. Therefore, statement III is false. Statements I and II, however, are both true. Since Aaron ran eight miles in eighty minutes, he ran an average of 1 mile every 10 minutes, or 6 miles every 60 minutes, which is 6 mph. He ran two miles from point (A) to (B) in 20 minutes, which is a rate of 1 mile per 10 minutes, and four miles from (D) to (E) in 40 minutes, which is also a rate of 1 mile per 10 minutes, so his running speed between both sets of points was the same.

8. A: Use the formula for the volume of a sphere to find the radius of the sphere:

$$\begin{aligned} V &= \frac{4}{3}\pi r^3 \\ 36\pi &= \frac{4}{3}\pi r^3 \\ 36 &= \frac{4}{3}r^3 \\ 27 &= r^3 \\ 3 &= r \end{aligned}$$

Then, substitute the point $(h, k, l) = (1, 0, -2)$ and the radius $r = 3$ into the equation of a sphere:

$$(x-h)^2 + (y-k)^2 + (z-l)^2 = r^2$$
$$(x-1)^2 + y^2 + (z+2)^2 = 3^2$$
$$(x-1)^2 + y^2 + (z+2)^2 = 9$$
$$x^2 - 2x + 1 + y^2 + z^2 + 4z + 4 = 9$$
$$x^2 + y^2 + z^2 - 2x + 4z = 4$$

9. C: There are $(n-1)!$ ways to arrange n units around a circle for $n > 1$. Because the teacher and Andrew must sit together, we can treat them as a unit, as though there were five people. So we calculate:

$$(n-1)! = (5-1)! = 4! = 24$$

There are 24 possible arrangements with Andrew and the teacher counted as a single unit. But for each of those, Andrew could be sitting either to her left or to her right, so we double the amount: $24 \times 2 = 48$.

10. A: The point $(-3, -16)$ lies on the line that has a slope of 3 and that passes through $(1, -4)$. If $(-3, -16)$ is one of the endpoints of the line, the other would be $(5, 8)$.

11. C: When a figure is reflected twice over non-parallel lines, the resulting transformation is a rotation about the point of intersection of the two lines of reflection. The two lines of reflection $y = x - 3$ and $x = 0$ intersect at $(0, -3)$. So, $\Delta A''B''C''$ represents a rotation of ΔABC about the point $(0, -3)$. The angle of rotation is equal to twice the angle between the two lines of reflection when measured in a counterclockwise direction from the first to the second line of reflection. Since the angle between the lines or reflection measures 45°, the angle of rotation equivalent to the composition of the two reflections measures 90°.

12. B: The slope of a straight line is a vital concept to understanding linear equations.

13. B: Euclidean geometry has five axioms: between any two points, a single, straight line segment may be drawn; any given right angle is congruent to any other right angle; straight line segments may be extended indefinitely; given a center point and a radius, a circle may be drawn; and if two lines are on a plane and intersected by another line, and if the internal angles on one side combine to less than two right angles, then the straight lines will eventually meet on the side where the angles combine to less than two right angles. Statement II is close to one of Euclid's axioms, but it is missing key information about being given a point and radius.

14. D: "The square of three times the sum of a and six is fourteen more than a" is represented by the equation $[3(a+6)]^2 = a + 14$. Solve for a.

$$[3a + 18]^2 = a + 14$$
$$9a^2 + 108a + 324 = a + 14$$
$$9a^2 + 107a + 310 = 0$$
$$(a+5)(9a+62) = 0$$
$$a = -5, -\frac{62}{9}$$

So, –5 is a possible value of a.

15. C: A height of 5'11", or 71 inches, is one standard deviation above the mean. Since approximately 68% of the data is within one standard deviation of the mean, about 32% (100% − 68%) of the data is outside of one standard deviation within the mean. Normally distributed data is symmetric about the mean, which means that about 16% of the data lies below one standard deviation below the mean and about 16% of data lies above one standard deviation above the mean. Therefore, approximately 16% of individuals are 5'11" or taller, while approximately 84% of the population is shorter than 5'11". Multiply to find 84% of 200, $0.84 \times 200 = 168$. So, about 168 people from the selected group are shorter than 5'11".

16. B: The set of rational numbers includes every number that can be written as quotient of two integers. Since $\sqrt{32}$ cannot be expressed as a fraction of integers, it is not a rational number, but it does fit in the sets of real and complex numbers.

17. D: First, gather the like terms on opposite sides of the equation.

$$\begin{aligned} -3q + 12 &\geq 4q - 30 \\ 12 &\geq 7q - 30 \\ 42 &\geq 7q \end{aligned}$$

Then, divide both sides by 7 to solve for q.

$$\begin{aligned} \frac{42}{7} &\geq \frac{7q}{7} \\ 6 &\geq q \end{aligned}$$

The inequality can be flipped to match the formatting of the answer choices, giving the inequality $q \leq 6$.

18. A: Since the figures are similar, the following proportion may be written and solved for x: $\frac{8}{6} = \frac{6}{x}$. Thus, $x = \frac{36}{8}$ or $4\frac{1}{2}$.

19. A: Calculate the final sales price of the rug at each store. Please note that the explanation below uses 1.08 instead of 0.08 for tax in order to avoid having to perform addition later. If 0.08 were to be used, only the amount of tax charged would result instead of the total cost of the product with tax included. Thus, 1.08 is used to make sure 108% of the product price is calculated.

$$\begin{aligned} 1.08(0.7 \times \$296) &= \$223.78 \text{ at Store A} \\ 1.08(\$220 - \$10) &= \$226.80 \text{ at Store B} \\ \$198 + \$35 &= \$233 \text{ at Store C} \end{aligned}$$

20. D: The angle $-\frac{2\pi}{3}$ is equivalent to $2\pi - \frac{2\pi}{3} = \frac{4\pi}{3}$.

$$\tan\left(-\frac{2\pi}{3}\right) = \tan\left(\frac{4\pi}{3}\right) = \frac{\sin\left(\frac{4\pi}{3}\right)}{\cos\left(\frac{4\pi}{3}\right)}$$

From the unit circle, the values of $\sin\left(\frac{4\pi}{3}\right)$ and $\cos\left(\frac{4\pi}{3}\right)$ are $-\frac{\sqrt{3}}{2}$ and $-\frac{1}{2}$, respectively. Substitute these values into the equation from above.

$$\tan\left(-\frac{2\pi}{3}\right) = \frac{-\frac{\sqrt{3}}{2}}{-\frac{1}{2}} = -\frac{\sqrt{3}}{2} \times -\frac{2}{1} = \sqrt{3}$$

Therefore, the value of $\tan\left(-\frac{2\pi}{3}\right)$ is $\sqrt{3}$.

21. B: First, use the properties of logarithms to solve for y:

$2\log_4 y + \log_4 16 = 3$	Write out the original equation.
$\log_4 y^2 + \log_4 16 = 3$	Use the power rule for logarithms: $\log_b(x^a) = a \cdot \log_b x$.
$\log_4 16y^2 = 3$	Then, use the product rule for logarithms: $\log_b x + \log_b y = \log_b(xy)$.
$16y^2 = 4^3$	Next, convert the logarithm to an exponential expression.
$16y^2 = 64$	Simplify the right side.
$y^2 = 4$	Divide both sides by 16.
$y = 2$	Take the positive square root of both sides.

Finally, substitute 2 for y in the expression $\log_y 256$ and simplify: $\log_2 256 = 8$ since $2^8 = 256$.

22. A: Since the graph shows a maximum height of 18 inches above the ground, and since the maximum distance from the road the pebble reaches occurs when it is at the top of the tire, the diameter of the tire is 18 inches. Therefore, its radius is 9 inches. From the graph, it can be observed that the tire makes 6 rotations in 1.5 seconds. Thus, the tire rotates 4 times in 1 second, or $4 \times 60 = 240$ times per minute.

23. A: The Babylonians used a base-60 numeral system, which is still used in the division of an hour into 60 minutes, a minute into 60 seconds, and a circle into 360 degrees. The word "algebra" and its development as a discipline separate from geometry are attributed to the Arabic/Islamic civilization. The Greek philosopher Thales is credited with using deductive reasoning to prove geometric concepts. Boolean logic was introduced by British mathematician George Boole.

24. B: In this sequence, 5 and 4 are added alternatively to successive numbers to determine the next numeral: $54 + 5 = 59$, $59 + 4 = 63$, etc. Since $68 + 4 = 72$, the next element is calculated by adding 5: $72 + 5 = 77$, so 77 is the next term in the sequence.

25. D: See the pattern from the table.

Years after purchase	0	1	2	3
Number of llamas	32	48	72	108

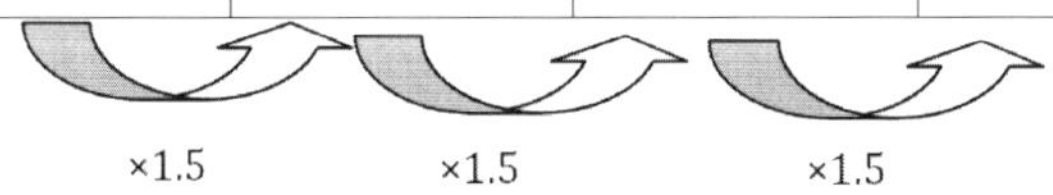

Multiplying 108 by 1.5 gives the predicted value 4 years after purchase $108 \times 1.5 = 162$.

26. A: 20 of the 38 sophomores taking an elective are male. The probability that a male is chosen is $\frac{\text{number of male sophomores}}{\text{number of sophomores}} = \frac{20}{38} \approx 0.53$.

27. A: The total number of students taking electives is 200, as seen in the chart on the right, and 16% of these are taking welding, so the number of students taking welding is $0.16 \times 200 = 32$. The number of male sophomores taking an elective is 20. The difference in the number of male and female students taking an elective is $108 - 92 = 16$. The difference in the number of juniors and seniors taking an elective is $83 - 59 = 24$. The greatest quantity of these is 32, the number of students taking welding.

28. C: ΔABC is similar to the smaller triangle with which it shares vertex B.

$$\overline{BC} = (2x - 2) + (x + 4) = 3x + 2$$
$$\overline{AB} = 3 + 9 = 12$$

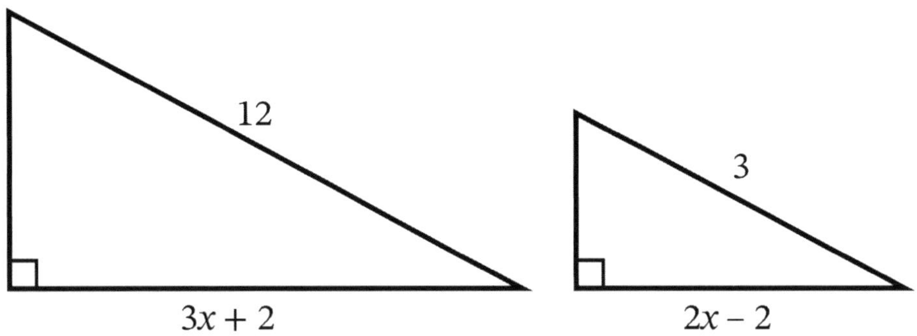

Set up a proportion and solve for x:

$$\frac{3x + 2}{12} = \frac{2x - 2}{3}$$
$$9x + 6 = 24x - 24$$
$$30 = 15x$$
$$x = 2$$

So, $BC = 3x + 2 = 3(2) + 2 = 8$.

29. D: First, add the two straight 150-yard portions. Also, note that the distance for the two semi-circles put together is the circumference of a circle. Since the circumference of a circle is π times the diameter, the length of the circular portion of the track is simply 30π. Then, add this to the length of the two straight portions of the track.

$$\text{Perimeter} = 30\pi + (2 \times 150) \approx 394.25$$

Therefore, the perimeter of the entire track is approximately 395 yards.

30. C: The problem does not give any information about the size of the table or the spacing between any of the chairs. Nevertheless, creating a simple illustration that shows the order of the chairs will help when approaching this problem. The line below shows the row of chairs and possible positions based on the parameters.

H J I L M K

Statements I and III seem to be true from the drawing, but since we are not given any information about the spacing between chairs, we cannot say definitively that H and L are farther apart than I and M, or that M and K are closer together than H and L. If the statement would have talked about the number of chairs between rather than distance, the statements would have also been true. However, we do know that chair I is between chairs J and L, so the only statement that is necessarily true is statement II.

31. B: The graph of $f(x)$ is a parabola with a focus of $(a, 3)$ and a directrix of $y = -1$. The axis of symmetry of a parabola passes through the focus and vertex and is perpendicular to the directrix. Since the directrix is a horizontal line, the axis of symmetry is $x = a$; therefore, the x-coordinate of the parabola's vertex must be a. The distance between a point on the parabola and the directrix is equal to the distance between that point and the focus, so the y-coordinate of the vertex must be $y = \frac{-1+3}{2} = 1$. So, the vertex of the parabola given by $f(x)$ is $(a, 1)$.

If $g(x)$ were a translation of $f(x)$, as is the case for choices B, C, and D, the vertices of $f(x)$ and $g(x)$ would differ. Since the vertex of the graph of $g(x)$ is $(a, 1)$, none of those choices represent the correct response. However, if $g(x) = 2f(x)$, the vertices of the graphs of both functions would be the same; therefore, this represents a possible relation between the two functions.

32. A: There are three ways in which two men from the same class can be selected: two men can be selected from the first class, or two men can be selected from the second class, or two men can be selected from the third class.

Class 1	**Class 2**	**Class 3**
$\frac{13}{93} \times \frac{12}{92} = \frac{156}{8{,}556}$	$\frac{14}{93} \times \frac{13}{92} = \frac{182}{8{,}556}$	$\frac{19}{93} \times \frac{18}{92} = \frac{342}{8{,}556}$

Since any of these is a distinct possible outcome, the probability that two men will be selected from the same class is the sum of these outcomes.

$$\frac{156}{8{,}556} + \frac{182}{8{,}556} + \frac{342}{8{,}556} = \frac{680}{8{,}556} \approx 0.079 = 7.9\%$$

The approximate probability that two men from the same class will be chosen is 7.9%.

33. D: Number lines can help students understand the concepts of positive and negative numbers. Fraction strips are most commonly used with fractions. Venn diagrams are commonly used when comparing groups. Shaded regions are commonly used with fractions or percentages.

34. B: Determine the probability of each option.

For choice A, this is the total number of students in the tea circle of the Venn diagram divided by the total number of students surveyed:

$$\frac{42 + 12 + 7 + 26}{250} = \frac{87}{250} = 34.8\%$$

For choice B, this is the total number of students in the hot chocolate circle and in at least one other circle divided by the total number in the hot chocolate circle:

$$\frac{31 + 7 + 26}{31 + 7 + 26 + 56} = \frac{64}{120} \approx 53.3\%$$

For choice C, this is the number of students in the intersection of all three circles divided by the total number in the overlap of the coffee and hot chocolate circles:

$$\frac{7}{7 + 31} = \frac{7}{38} \approx 18.4\%$$

For choice D, this is the number of students outside of all the circles divided by the total number of students surveyed:

$$\frac{11}{250} = 4.4\%$$

Choice B has the greatest probability.

35. C: The teacher should be most concerned that several students in her classroom struggled with an assignment so much that they were unable to complete it. When something like this happens in the classroom, a teacher should be willing to self-assess what they may have done incorrectly, or what they could do differently in the future. A teacher should ensure that activities and assignments in their classroom are able to be completed by all students in their classroom, even if some students may need some accommodations due to disabilities or other limitations. The goal of education is to make learning accessible for all students, and that should be one of a teacher's most important goals in the classroom.

36. C: The interior angles of a trapezoid add up to 360°. The two larger angles on each trapezoid are congruent and are equal to $x - 24°$. The other two angles add up to x, as shown on the far right. So, $x - 24 + x - 24 + x = 360$. Solve for x:

$$\begin{aligned} x - 24 + x - 24 + x &= 360 \\ 3x - 48 &= 360 \\ 3x &= 408 \\ x &= 136° \end{aligned}$$

37. D: Before you can solve a problem, you must decide what it is asking.

38. A: A pie chart shows the relationship of parts to a whole. A line graph is often used to show change over time. A box-and-whisker plot displays how numeric data are distributed throughout the range. A Venn diagram shows the relationships among sets. Therefore, a pie chart would best illustrate the percentage of a budget allocated to various departments.

39. B: A quick estimate of the total miles can be obtained by rounding each leg of the trip to the nearest whole mile and finding the sum: $5 + 7 + 14 + 15 = 41$ miles.

40. B: Percent error $= \frac{|\text{actual value} - \text{measured value}|}{\text{actual value}} \times 100\%$, and the average percent error is the sum of the percent errors for each trial divided by the number of trials.

	Percent Error Trial 1	Percent Error Trial 2	Percent Error Trial 3	Percent Error Trial 4	Average Percent Error
Scale 1	0.1%	0.2%	0.2%	0.1%	0.15%
Scale 2	2.06%	2.09%	2.10%	2.08%	2.08%

The percent error for Scale 1 is less than the percent error for Scale 2, so it is more accurate. The more precise scale is Scale 2 because its range of values, $10.210 \text{ g} - 10.206 \text{ g} = 0.004 \text{ g}$, is smaller than the Scale 2's range of values, $10.02 \text{ g} - 9.98 \text{ g} = 0.04 \text{ g}$.

41. B: First, set the equation equal to zero, then factor it.

$$\begin{aligned} 4x^3y^2 - 16x^2y &= -16x^3y + 4x^2y^2 \\ 4x^3y^2 + 16x^3y - 4x^2y^2 - 16x^2y &= 0 \\ 4x^2y(xy + 4x - y - 4) &= 0 \\ 4x^2y[x(y + 4) - 1(y + 4)] &= 0 \\ 4x^2y[(y + 4)(x - 1)] &= 0 \end{aligned}$$

Use the zero-product property to find the solution. Since the question only asks to solve for x, only look at the terms that have x in them.

$$\begin{aligned} 4x^2y &= 0 & \qquad x - 1 &= 0 \\ x &= 0 & x &= 1 \end{aligned}$$

So, the solutions are $x = \{0,1\}$.

42. D: Alex is incorrectly regrouping when multiplying. If Alex continues to use this incorrect regrouping strategy for the problem 174×2, the result will be 2,148, as illustrated below.

$$\begin{array}{r} 174 \\ \times\ 2 \\ \hline 2{,}148 \end{array}$$

In order to address the error, Alex needs to regroup the 14. The product of 174 × 2 should be 348, as illustrated below.

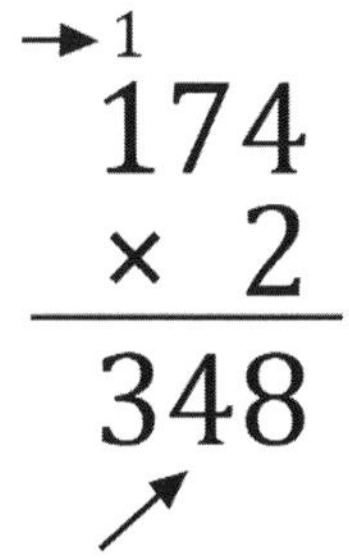

When a product is greater than 9, the tens value needs to be carried over to the next column to the left. For example, on #1, Alex correctly records 3 × 3 as 9. However, when recording 3 × 4, Alex incorrectly places both digits of the product in the answer line. The product of 12 should have been regrouped as shown below.

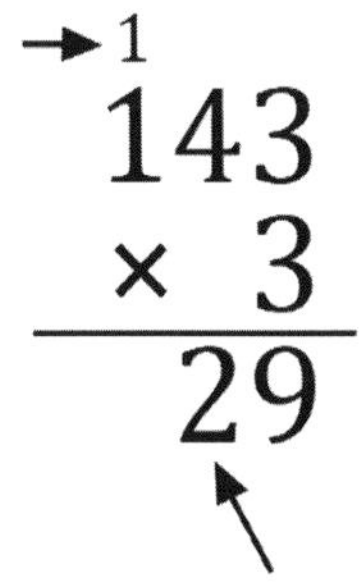

After regrouping the 12, the problem can continue. 3 × 1 is 3, plus the 1 (from regrouping) equals 4. The final answer should be 429.

$$\begin{array}{r} ^{1} \\ 143 \\ \times\ 3 \\ \hline 429 \end{array}$$

43. B: First, simplify the expression by expanding the squared binomial.

$$(4 - i)^2 - (2 - 4i)$$
$$(4 - i)(4 - i) - (2 - 4i)$$
$$(16 - 8i + i^2) - (2 - 4i)$$

Then, distribute the negative sign and combine like terms.

$$16 - 8i + i^2 - 2 + 4i$$
$$14 - 4i + i^2$$

Remember, $i^2 = -1$, so substitute this value into the expression and combine like terms once more.

$$14 - 4i - 1$$
$$13 - 4i$$

44. C: The area of a triangle is $A = \frac{1}{2}bh$, where b and h are the lengths of the triangle's base and height, respectively. The base of the given triangle is 8, but the height is not given. Since the triangle is a right triangle and the hypotenuse is given, the triangle's height can be found using the Pythagorean theorem.

$$8^2 + h^2 = x^2$$
$$h^2 = x^2 - 8^2$$
$$h^2 = x^2 - 64$$
$$h = \sqrt{x^2 - 64}$$

To find the area of the triangle in terms of x, substitute $\sqrt{x^2 - 64}$ for the height and 8 for the base of the triangle into the area formula ($A = \frac{1}{2}bh$):

$$A(x) = \frac{1}{2}(8)(\sqrt{x^2 - 64})$$
$$A(x) = 4\sqrt{x^2 - 64}$$

45. D: Since there are 100 cm in a meter, on a 1 : 100 scale drawing, each centimeter represents one meter. Therefore, an area of one square centimeter on the drawing represents one square meter in actuality. Since the area of the room in the scale drawing is 30 cm^2, the room's actual area is 30 m^2.

Another way to determine the area of the room is to write and solve an equation, such as this one: $\frac{l}{100} \times \frac{w}{100} = 30 \text{ cm}^2$, where l and w are the dimensions of the actual room.

$$\frac{lw}{10{,}000} = 30 \text{ cm}^2$$
$$\text{Area} = 300{,}000 \text{ cm}^2$$

Since this is not one of the answer choices, convert cm^2 to m^2.

$$300{,}000 \text{ cm}^2 \times \frac{1 \text{ m}}{100 \text{ cm}} \times \frac{1 \text{ m}}{100 \text{ cm}} = 30 \text{ m}^2$$

46. D: 131 of 283 eleventh graders are male. It is given that an eleventh grader is chosen to attend the conference, so the probability that a male is chosen is $\frac{\text{number of 11th grade males}}{\text{number of 11th graders}} = \frac{131}{283} \approx 0.46$.

47. D: One way to determine whether the equation represents an ellipse, a circle, a parabola, or a hyperbola is to find the discriminant $b^2 - 4ac$ of the general equation form of a conic section, $ax^2 + bxy + cy^2 + dx + ey + f = 0$, where a, b, c, d, e, and f are constants. Given that the conic section is non-degenerate, if the discriminant is positive, then the equation is a hyperbola; if the discriminant is negative, then the equation is a circle (when $a = c$ and $b = 0$) or an ellipse; and if the discriminant is zero, then the equation is a parabola. For $2x^2 - 3y^2 - 12x + 6y - 15 = 0$, $a = 2, b = 0, c = -3, d = -12, e = 6$, and $f = -15$. The discriminant $b^2 - 4ac$ is equal to $0^2 - 4(2)(-3) = 24$. Since the discriminant is positive, the graph is hyperbolic.

48. B: It is necessary to find the area of the floor by multiplying the dimensions together. However, since the dimensions are given in feet and we only know the price of carpeting per square yard, converting the dimensions from feet to yards first is helpful. Since there are 3 feet in a yard, dividing each of the dimensions by 3 will give us the measurements in yards.

$$18 \div 3 = 6$$
$$27 \div 3 = 9$$

So, the floor is 6 yards by 9 yards, which is an area of 54 square yards. Last, we multiply 54 by 14, since each square yard costs $14 and there are 54 square yards.

$$54 \times 14 = 756$$

So, the price of the carpet should be $756.

49. A: Nominal data are data that are collected which have no intrinsic quantity or order. For instance, a survey might ask the respondent to identify his or her gender. While it is possible to compare the relative frequency of each response (for example, "most of the respondents are women"), it is not possible to calculate the mean, which requires data to be numeric, or median, which requires data to be ordered. Interval data are both numeric and ordered, so mean and median can be determined, as can the mode, the interval within which there are the most data. Ordinal data has an inherent order, but there is not a set interval between two points. For example, a survey might ask the respondents whether they were very dissatisfied, dissatisfied, neutral, satisfied, or very satisfied with the customer service received. Since the data are not numeric, the mean cannot be calculated, but since ordering the data is possible, the median has context.

50. A: Since the y-coordinates of points P and Q are the same, line segment $\overline{PQ}$ is a horizontal line segment whose length is the difference in the x-coordinates a and c. Because the length of a line cannot be negative, and because it is unknown whether $a > c$ or $a < c$, $PQ = |a - c|$ or $|c - a|$. Since the x-coordinates of Q and P' are the same, line segment $\overline{P'Q}$ is a vertical line segment whose length is $|d - b|$ or $|b - d|$. The quadrilateral formed by the transformation of $\overline{PQ}$ to $\overline{P'Q'}$ is a parallelogram. If the base of the parallelogram is $\overline{PQ}$, then the height is $\overline{P'Q}$ since $\overline{PQ} \perp \overline{P'Q}$. For a parallelogram, $A = bh$, so $A = |a - c| \times |b - d|$.

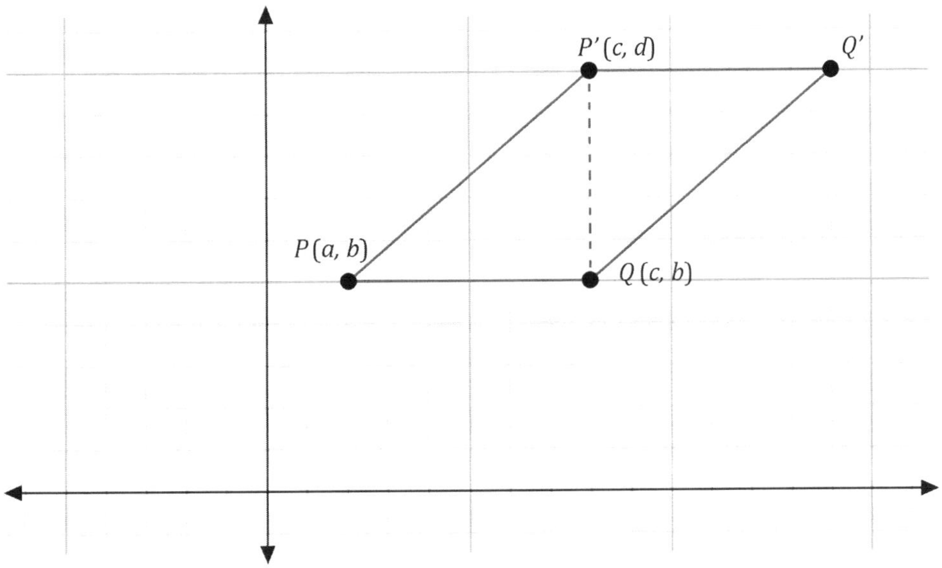

51. B: To find the integral, use u-substitution. Since the derivative and integral of e^x is itself but this function has e raised to a power, use the power as u when doing u-substitution.

$$\int 3x^2 e^{x^3}\,dx \quad \text{Let } u = x^3;\ du = 3x^2 dx$$

$$\int e^u\,du = e^u + C$$
$$= e^{x^3} + C$$

52. C: The distance that is being traveled and the speed are known. If we let the number of hours the trip will take be x, then we can solve the problem in the following way:

$$\begin{aligned} distance &= speed \times time \\ 827\text{ km} &= 64\,\frac{\text{km}}{\text{hr}} \times x \\ \frac{827\text{ km}}{64\,\frac{\text{km}}{\text{hr}}} &= x \\ 12.92\text{ hours} &= x \end{aligned}$$

Rounding off, we get 13 hours.

53. B: Graphically, a relationship between x and y can be identified as a function if the graph passes the vertical line test. Choice B is the graph of $y = x^3$, which is a function because it passes the vertical line test. A function is a relationship in which for every element of the domain (x) produces exactly one element of the range (y).

The first relation is a circle, which fails the vertical line test for functions. Choice C is a parabola on its side, which also fails the vertical line test and is therefore not a function. The relation in choice D has an element of the domain (2) that maps to two different range values, so it is also not a function.

54. C: Formative assessment refers to any kind of evaluation by a teacher that helps guide her instruction. In mathematics instruction, teachers need to know exactly what the students have mastered in order to teach them appropriately because so many principles must be taught consecutively and in appropriate order. Conversations, class work and homework are all examples of formative assessments. These practices help teachers know where students might need more help and where instruction should be focused.

55. B: The sine function is represented by the ratio $\frac{\text{opposite leg}}{\text{hypotenuse}}$. So, the sine of angle A can be written as $\frac{BC}{AB}$. The cosine function is represented by the ratio $\frac{\text{adjacent leg}}{\text{hypotenuse}}$. In ΔABC, $\cos B$ can also be written as $\frac{BC}{AB}$. We can also determine that angle B is 62°. Since the two acute angles of a right triangle are complementary, we can find that angle A is $90 - 62 = 28°$. Since we can see that the sine of angle A is equal to the cosine of angle B, we know that the cosine of angle A will also be equal to the sine of angle B. So $\cos A = \sin B = \sin 62°$.

56. D: Since there are 100 homes' market times represented in each set, the median time a home spends on the market is between the 50th and 51st data point in each set. The 50th and 51st data points for Zip Code 1 are six months and seven months, respectively, so the median time a house in Zip Code 1 spends on the market is between six and seven months (6.5 months), which by the realtor's definition of market time is a seven-month market time. The 50th and 51st data points for Zip Code 2 are both thirteen months, so the median time a house in Zip Code 2 spends on the market is thirteen months. Therefore, there is a six-month difference between the median of Zip Code 1 and the median of Zip Code 2.

To find the mean market time for 100 houses, find the sum of the market times and divide by 100. If the frequency of a one-month market time is 9, the number 1 is added nine times (1×9), if the frequency of a two-month market time is 10, the number 2 is added ten times (2×10), and so on. So, to find the average market time, divide by 100 the sum of the products of each market time and its corresponding frequency. For Zip Code 1, the mean market time is 7.38 months, which, by the realtor's definition of market time, is an eight-month market time. For Zip Code 2, the mean market time is 12.74, which, by the realtor's definition of market time, is a thirteen-month market time. Therefore, the difference between the mean of Zip Code 1 and the mean of Zip Code 2 is 5 months.

The mode market time is the market time for which the frequency is the highest. For Zip Code 1, the mode market time is three months, and for Zip Code 2, the mode market time is eleven months. Therefore, the median time a house spends on the market in Zip Code 1 is less than the mean time a house spends on the market in Zip Code 1.

57. D: Bacterial growth is exponential. Let x be the number of times the population doubles, a be the number of bacteria in the colony originally transferred into the broth, and y be the number of bacteria in the broth after x doubling times. After 1 hour, the population would have doubled three times:

$$a(2)^x = y$$
$$a(2^3) = 8 \times 10^6$$
$$8a = 8 \times 10^6$$
$$a = 10^6$$

So, the number of bacteria originally transferred into the petri dish was 10^6. The equation for determining the number of bacteria is $y = (2^x) \times 10^6$. Since the bacteria double every twenty minutes, they go through three doubling times every hour. So, when the bacteria are allowed to grow for eight hours, they will have gone through $8 \times 3 = 24$ doubling times. When $x = 24$, $y = (2^{24}) \times 10^6 = 16{,}777{,}216 \times 10^6$, which is approximately 1.7×10^{13}.

58. C: The recursive definition of the sequence gives the first term of the series, $a_1 = -2$. The definition also defines each term in the series as the sum of the previous term and $\frac{1}{2}$. Therefore, the second term in the series is $-2 + \frac{1}{2} = -\frac{3}{2}$, the third term in the series is $-\frac{3}{2} + \frac{1}{2} = -1$, and so on.

n	a_n
1	-2
2	$-\frac{3}{2}$
3	-1

The relationship between n and a_n is linear, so the equation of the sequence can be found in the same way as the equation of a line. The value of a_n increases by $\frac{1}{2}$ each time the value of n increases by 1.

n	$\frac{n}{2}$	a_n
1	$\frac{1}{2}$	-2
2	1	$-\frac{3}{2}$
3	$\frac{3}{2}$	-1

Since the difference between $\frac{1}{2}n$ and a_n is $-\frac{5}{2}$. So, $a_n = \frac{1}{2}n - \frac{5}{2}$.

n	$\frac{n}{2} - \frac{5}{2}$	a_n
1	$\frac{1}{2} - \frac{5}{2}$	-2
2	$1 - \frac{5}{2}$	$-\frac{3}{2}$
3	$\frac{3}{2} - \frac{5}{2}$	-1

59. B: The table shows a pattern that the number of wolves is multiplied by 1.5 each year.

Years after release	0	1	2	3	4
Number of wolves	16	24	36	54	81

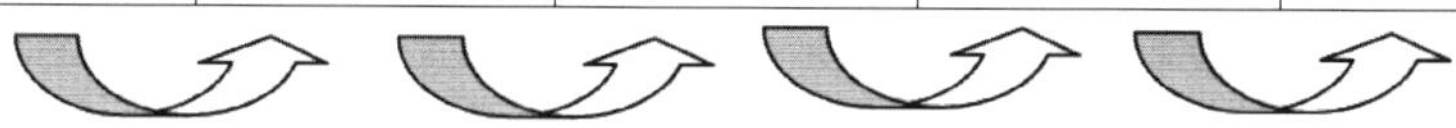

× 1.5 × 1.5 × 1.5 × 1.5

60. D: If the statement is written in the form $p \rightarrow q$, then the converse is represented as $q \rightarrow p$. Thus, the converse should read, "If it is spring, I see a robin."

61. A: First, subtract the matrices in parentheses, then multiply the resulting matrices together.

$$\begin{aligned}[2 \quad 0 \quad -5]\begin{bmatrix}(4-3)\\(2-5)\\(-1-(-5))\end{bmatrix} &= [2 \quad 0 \quad -5]\begin{bmatrix}1\\-3\\4\end{bmatrix}\\ &= [(2)(1)+(0)(-3)+(-5)(4)]\\ &= [-18]\end{aligned}$$

Note that the product of a 1×3 matrix and a 3×1 matrix, in that order, is a 1×1 matrix. If the order was reversed, the product would be a 3×3 matrix.

62. A: The set of whole numbers, $\{0, 1, 2, 3, \dots\}$, does not contain the number –4. Since –4 is an integer, it is also a rational number and a real number.

63. C: The length of the fence is equal to the perimeter of the rectangular property. The perimeter of the property is equal to the sum of twice the length and twice the width. The length is approximately 400 feet, and the width is approximately 300 feet, so the perimeter is $2(400) + 2(300) = 1{,}400$ feet.

64. B: The average number of females per age bracket is the total number of females divided by 4, or $\frac{297}{4} = 74.25$. The number of volunteers at the animal shelter is 13% of the total number of volunteers (626), which is $0.13(626) = 81.38$. The difference in the number of male and female volunteers is $329 - 297 = 32$, and the difference in the number of people over 60 and people under 21 is $187 - 118 = 69$. The greatest quantity of the answer choices is the number of volunteers at the animal shelter.

65. C: 65 of 118 volunteers under the age of 21 are male. So, the probability that a male is chosen is $\frac{\text{number of 0–20 year–old males}}{\text{number of 0–20 year–olds}} = \frac{65}{118} \approx 0.55$.

66. C: Printed mathematical formulas are an example of abstract mathematical concepts presented abstractly. Young children cannot access such concepts in abstract presentations. However, they can learn to understand abstract concepts when they are presented using concrete manipulatives like tangrams for shape recognition (A), or for reproducing and designing patterns, solving spatial problems, etc.; large, magnetized numbers and number boards (B) for doing math computations concretely; play money and toy cash registers (D) for monetary numerical activities; linking cubes, color tiles; and many other math manipulatives, which are available for teachers/schools to purchase, and/or which teachers can create in homemade versions using commonly found objects.

67. B: A simple test of each option at $x = -5$, $x = 0$, and $x = 2$ demonstrates that only choice B works:

x	**Observed**	y_a	y_b	y_c	y_d
-5	$\sim\mathbf{\frac{1}{6}}$	-2	$\frac{1}{6}$	$-\frac{7}{6}$	$\frac{1}{9}$
0	$\sim-\mathbf{\frac{1}{4}}$	$\frac{1}{2}$	$-\frac{1}{4}$	$-\frac{3}{4}$	$-\frac{1}{6}$
2	$\sim\mathbf{\frac{1}{6}}$	$\frac{1}{3}$	$\frac{1}{6}$	$\frac{7}{6}$	$\frac{1}{9}$

68. D: Being aware that patterns (regular repetitions) and relationships (associations between/among things) exist in the world affords us greater self-efficacy about our interacting with the environment, as well as increases our sense of confidence in the environment itself (C). This awareness not only helps us to understand sequences of events; it moreover enables us to predict the next event in the series before it occurs (B). Having an awareness of patterns and relationships in things also informs our understanding of the basic structure of those things (A).

69. B: Choice B does not simulate random selection because the probability of different outcomes is not equal. For instance, there is only one combination of dice outcomes that can produce the value 2 or 12, whereas there are several combinations that produce the value of 7.

70. D: We tend not only to see or impose patterns and relationships where they do not objectively exist (like seeing animal, human, and object shapes in the clouds); we also deliberately create patterns and relationships in the works of art (A), pieces of music (B), and articles of clothing (C) we produce. We also notice and appreciate the patterns and relationships in these products that others have created.

71. D: On the unit circle, $\sin\theta = \frac{1}{2}$ when $\theta = \frac{\pi}{6}$ and when $\theta = \frac{5\pi}{6}$. Since only $\frac{5\pi}{6}$ satisfies the condition $\frac{\pi}{2} < \theta < \pi$, this means that $\theta = \frac{5\pi}{6}$.

72. B: Frequent evaluations show how students perform on a weekly or daily basis. Moreover, they often reveal problems earlier enough that they can be effectively address without ruining the student's grades. Answer A is not always reliable since a student may be nervous or not functioning at his/her best on the particular day of the test. Answer C is nonsense. A teacher's evaluation should always be based on objective indicators. Answer D can certainly be useful, but these assignments do not indicate how a student performs under controlled conditions and without access to references such as calculators, encyclopedias, or help from family members.

73. D: A system of linear equations can be solved by using matrices or by using the graphing, substitution, or elimination method. The elimination method is shown here.

$$\begin{cases} -4x + 3y = 8 \\ 6x - 2y = -7 \end{cases}$$

To eliminate y by the elimination method, multiply the top equation by 2 and the bottom equation by 3 so that the coefficients of the y-terms will be additive inverses.

$$2(-4x + 3y) = (8)2 \qquad\qquad 3(6x - 2y) = (-7)(3)$$
$$-8x + 6y = 16 \qquad\qquad 18x - 6y = -21$$

Then, add the two equations and solve for x.

$$\begin{array}{rrcr} -8x & +6y & = & 16 \\ +\ 18x & -6y & = & -21 \\ \hline & 10x & = & -5 \\ & x & = & -\frac{1}{2} \end{array}$$

Substitute $-\frac{1}{2}$ for x in either of the given equations and solve for y.

$$\begin{aligned} -4x + 3y &= 8 \\ -4\left(-\frac{1}{2}\right) + 3y &= 8 \\ 2 + 3y &= 8 \\ 3y &= 6 \\ y &= 2 \end{aligned}$$

The solution to the system of equations is $\left(-\frac{1}{2}, 2\right)$.

74. B: In the range $(-\infty, -2)$, the graph represented is $y = -x + 1$. In the range $[-2,1)$, the graph is a form of the greatest integer function, shifted one space to the left, $y = [\![x + 1]\!]$. In the range $[1, \infty)$, the graph is $y = -x + 3$.

75. C: The sequence consists of the squares of consecutive integers, beginning with 1: $1^2 = 1$, $2^2 = 4$, $3^2 = 9$, and $4^2 = 16$. In the fifth position, $5^2 = 25$, so 25 is the next number.

76. D: Consider each answer choice. The x-intercept is the point at which $f(x) = 0$. When $0 = \log_b x$, $b^0 = x$; since $b^0 = 1$, the x-intercept of $f(x) = \log_b x$ is always 1. If $f(x) = \log_b x$ and $x = b$, then $f(x) = \log_b b$, which is, by definition, 1 ($b^1 = b$). The statement $f(x) < 0$ is true only for x-values between 0 and 1. Choice D states, "If $g(x) = x^b$, the graph of $f(x)$ is symmetric to the graph of $g(x)$ with respect to $y = x$." This is a false statement. On the other hand, if $g(x) = b^x$, then $f(x)$ and $g(x)$ are inverse functions and are therefore symmetric with respect to $y = x$.

77. B: Notice that $x = 1$ results in a zero in the denominator, so choice C cannot be correct since $x \neq 1$. To solve, subtract $\frac{2}{x-1}$ from both sides, then cross-multiply.

$\frac{x-2}{x-1} = \frac{x-1}{x+1} + \frac{2}{x-1}$	Write out the original equation.
$\frac{x-4}{x-1} = \frac{x-1}{x+1}$	Subtract $\frac{2}{x-1}$ from both sides.
$(x+1)(x-4) = (x-1)(x-1)$	Cross multiply.
$x^2 - 3x - 4 = x^2 - 2x + 1$	Multiply the binomials on both sides.
$-3x - 4 = -2x + 1$	Subtract x^2 from both sides.
$-4 = x + 1$	Add $3x$ to both sides.
$-5 = x$	Subtract 1 from both sides.

78. B: Rate in miles per hour can be expressed as, mph $= \frac{\text{distance in miles}}{\text{time in hours}}$. So, Zeke's driving speed on the way to Atlanta and home from Atlanta in mph can be expressed as $\frac{d}{3}$ and $\frac{d}{2}$, respectively, where d is the distance between Zeke's house and his destination. Since Zeke drove 20 mph faster on his way home, (speed home) − (speed to store) = 20. Substitute Zeke's speeds and solve for d.

$$\frac{d}{2} - \frac{d}{3} = 20$$

$$6\left(\frac{d}{2} - \frac{d}{3} = 20\right)$$
$$3d - 2d = 120$$
$$d = 120$$

Since the distance between Zeke's house and the store in Atlanta is 120 miles, Zeke drove a total distance of 240 miles in five hours. Therefore, his average speed was $\frac{240 \text{ miles}}{5 \text{ hours}} = 48$ mph.

79. C: The approximate price of the fence is found by rounding to 70 feet at \$4 per foot.

$$\text{Price} = 70 \text{ ft} \times \$4/\text{ft} = \$280$$

Therefore, he will spend approximately \$280 on fencing. The actual price is 71 ft × \$3.98/ft = \$282.58.

80. C: If x is a prime number and the greatest common factor of x and y is greater than 1, the greatest common factor of x and y must be x. The least common multiple of two numbers is equal to the product of those numbers divided by their greatest common factor. So, the least common multiple of x and y is $\frac{xy}{x} = y$. Therefore, the two quantities are the same.

81. B: The series is an infinite geometric series, the sum of which can be found by using the formula $\sum_{n=0}^{\infty} ar^n = \frac{a}{1-r}, |r| < 1$ where a is the first term in the series and r is the ratio between successive terms. In the series $200 + 100 + 50 + 25 + \cdots$, $a = 200$ and $r = \frac{1}{2}$. So, the sum of the series is:

$$\frac{200}{1-\frac{1}{2}} = \frac{200}{\frac{1}{2}} = 400$$

82. A: Setting the cost of shipping equal to the amount received gives us the equation $3{,}000 + 100x = 400x$. Subtract $100x$ from both sides to get $3{,}000 = 300x$, then divide both sides by 300 to see that $x = 10$. Therefore, the least number of computers that must be shipped and sold is 10.

83. B: If each of the 4 groups in the class of 20 will contain 3 boys and 2 girls, there must be 12 boys and 8 girls in the class. The number of ways the teacher can select 3 boys from a group of 12 boys is:

$${}_{12}C_3 = \frac{12!}{3!\,(12-3)!} = \frac{12!}{3!\,9!} = \frac{12 \times 11 \times 10 \times 9!}{3!\,9!} = \frac{12 \times 11 \times 10}{3 \times 2 \times 1} = 220$$

The number of ways she can select 2 girls from a group of 8 girls is:

$${}_{8}C_2 = \frac{8!}{2!\,(8-2)!} = \frac{8!}{2!\,6!} = \frac{8 \times 7 \times 6!}{2!\,6!} = \frac{8 \times 7}{2 \times 1} = 28$$

Since each combination of boys can be paired with each combination of girls, the number of group combinations is $220 \times 28 = 6{,}160$.

84. B: If $f(x) = 10^x$ and $f(x) = 1$, then $1 = 10^x$. Any number to a power of 0 equals 1, so $10^0 = 1$ and $x = 0$.

85. C: The expression representing the charge for Ride Service A is $\$10 + \$0.25(m - 10)$, where m is the number of miles. Set this expression equal to the charge for Ride Service B, which is $\$0.40m$. Solve for m to find the number of miles the two companies charge the same amount.

$$\begin{aligned} \$10 + \$0.25(m - 10) &= \$0.40m \\ \$10 + \$0.25m - \$2.50 &= \$0.40m \\ \$7.50 &= \$0.15m \\ m &= 50 \end{aligned}$$

So, the cost of the two services would be the same for a 50-mile ride.

86. B: The volume of Natasha's tent can be found by using the volume formula for a square pyramid, $V = \frac{1}{3}Bh = \frac{1}{3}s^2h$, where B is the area of the base, s is the side length of the square base, and h is the height of the pyramid. Therefore, the volume of her tent is $\frac{x^2h}{3}$. If she were to increase the length of each side of the square base by 1 ft, the tent's volume would be $\frac{(x+1)^2h}{3} = \frac{(x^2+2x+1)(h)}{3} = \frac{x^2h+2xh+h}{3} = \frac{x^2h}{3} + \frac{2xh+h}{3}$. Notice this is the volume of Natasha's tent, $\frac{x^2h}{3}$, increased by $\frac{2xh+h}{3}$.

87. A: First, state the exclusions of the domain.

$$x^3 + 3x^2 - 6x - 8 \neq 0$$
$$(x-2)(x+4)(x+1) \neq 0$$
$$x - 2 \neq 0 \quad x + 4 \neq 0 \quad x + 1 \neq 0$$
$$x \neq 2 \quad x \neq -4 \quad x \neq -1$$

To determine whether there are asymptotes or holes at these values of x, simplify the expression:

$$\frac{x^2 - 2x - 3}{x^3 + 3x^2 - 6x - 8} = \frac{(x-3)(x+1)}{(x-2)(x+4)(x+1)} = \frac{x-3}{(x-2)(x+4)}$$

There are asymptotes at $x = 2$ and at $x = -4$ and a hole at $x = -1$. Statement I is true.

To find the x-intercept of $f(x)$, solve $f(x) = 0$. $f(x) = 0$ when the numerator is equal to zero. The numerator equals zero when $x = 3$ and $x = -1$; however, -1 is excluded from the domain of $f(x)$, so the x-intercept is 3. To find the y-intercept of $f(x)$, find $f(0)$.

$$\frac{0^2 - 2(0) - 3}{0^3 + 3(0)^2 - 6(0) - 8} = \frac{-3}{-8} = \frac{3}{8}$$

The x-intercept is 3, but the y-intercept is not 3. Statement II is false.

88. A: If $\cos\theta + 1 = 0$, then $\cos\theta = -1$. This has only one solution in the interval $0° \leq \theta < 360°$, namely $\theta = 180°$. This is not one of the answer choices; however, the cosine function has a period of 360°, which means that adding or subtracting any multiple of 360° to the argument does not change the result. Since $180° - 360° = -180°$, $\cos(-180°) = \cos(180°) = -1$, so $-180°$ is also a solution to the equation.

89. A: If $y = -a(x+b)(x+c)^2$, the degree of the polynomial is 3. Since the degree of the polynomial is odd and the leading coefficient is negative ($a < 0$), the end behavior of the graph goes to $(\infty, -\infty)$ and $(-\infty, \infty)$. Therefore, only Choice A is a possible graph of this function.

90. B: First, state the exclusions of the domain. This can be done by factoring the denominator, then finding where the denominator is equal to 0.

$$x^3 + 2x^2 - x - 2 \neq 0$$
$$x^2(x+2) - (x+2) \neq 0$$
$$(x+2)(x^2-1) \neq 0$$
$$(x+2)(x-1)(x+1) \neq 0$$
$$x+2 \neq 0 \quad x-1 \neq 0 \quad x+1 \neq 0$$
$$x \neq -2 \qquad x \neq 1 \qquad x \neq -1$$

To determine whether there are vertical asymptotes or holes at these values of x, simplify the expression:

$$\frac{x^2 - x - 6}{x^3 + 2x^2 - x - 2} = \frac{(x-3)(x+2)}{(x+2)(x-1)(x+1)} = \frac{x-3}{(x-1)(x+1)}$$

There are vertical asymptotes at $x = 1$ and at $x = -1$ and a hole at $x = -2$. Statement I is false.

To find the x-intercept of $f(x)$, solve $f(x) = 0$. $f(x) = 0$ when the numerator is equal to zero.

$$x^2 - x - 6 = 0$$
$$(x+2)(x-3) = 0$$
$$x = -2, 3$$

The numerator equals zero when $x = -2$ and $x = 3$; however, –2 is excluded from the domain of $f(x)$, so the x-intercept is 3. To find the y-intercept of $f(x)$, find $f(0)$.

$$\frac{(0)^2 - (0) - 6}{(0)^3 + 2(0)^2 - (0) - 2} = \frac{-6}{-2} = 3$$

The y-intercept is 3. Statement II is true.

91. B: A cube has six square faces. The arrangement of these faces in a two-dimensional figure is a net of a cube if the figure can be folded to form a cube. If choice B is folded, the bottom square in the second column will overlap the fourth square in the top row, so the figure does not represent a net of a cube. The other figures represent three of the eleven possible nets of a cube.

92. C: Find the missing angle measures in the diagram by using angle and triangle properties. Then, use the law of sines to find the distance y between the window and the wife's car: $\frac{60}{\sin 15°} = \frac{y}{\sin 45°}$, so $y = \frac{60 \sin 45°}{\sin 15°} \approx 163.9$ ft. Use this number in a sine or cosine function to find x: $\sin 30° \approx \frac{x}{163.9}$, so

$x \approx 163.9 \sin 30° \approx 82$. Therefore, the man's wife is parked approximately 82 feet from the building.

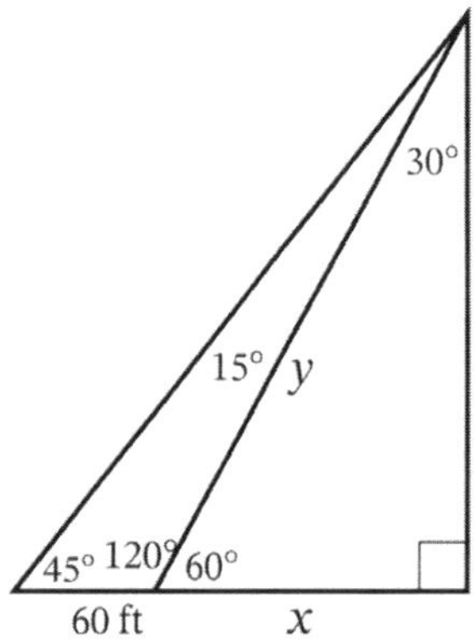

Alternatively, notice that when the man is looking down at a 45-degree angle, the triangle that is formed is an isosceles triangle, meaning that the height of his office is the same as the distance from the office to his car, or $x + 60$ feet. With this knowledge, the problem can be modeled with a single equation.

$$\frac{x+60}{x} = \tan 60°$$
$$x + 60 = x \tan 60°$$
$$60 = x \tan 60° - x$$
$$60 = x(\tan 60° - 1)$$
$$\frac{60}{\tan 60° - 1} = x$$
$$82 \approx x$$

With both methods of solving, the wife's car is approximately 82 feet from the building.

93. D: Solve this equation by completing the square or by using the quadratic formula, $x = \frac{-b \pm \sqrt{b^2 - 4ac}}{2a}$. Here we will use the quadratic formula. First, set the equation equal to 0 by adding 2 to both sides. The equation $5x^2 - 4x + 2 = 0$ has $a = 5, b = -4, c = 2$. Substitute these values into the quadratic formula and simplify.

$$x = \frac{-b \pm \sqrt{b^2 - 4ac}}{2a}$$
$$x = \frac{4 \pm \sqrt{(-4)^2 - 4(5)(2)}}{2(5)}$$
$$x = \frac{4 \pm \sqrt{16 - 40}}{10}$$
$$x = \frac{4 \pm \sqrt{-24}}{10}$$
$$x = \frac{4 \pm 2i\sqrt{6}}{10}$$
$$x = \frac{2 \pm i\sqrt{6}}{5}$$

94. D: To simplify, get as many terms as possible out from the radical as possible. Then, rationalize the denominator to remove any radicals from the denominator.

$$\sqrt{\frac{-54x^5}{80y^6}} = \sqrt{\frac{-9x^4 \times (6x)}{16y^6 \times (5)}}$$
$$= \sqrt{\frac{-(3x^2)^2 \times (6x)}{(4y^3)^2 \times (5)}}$$
$$= \frac{3x^2 i\sqrt{6x}}{4y^3\sqrt{5}} \times \frac{\sqrt{5}}{\sqrt{5}}$$
$$= \frac{3x^2 i\sqrt{30x}}{20y^3}$$

95. C: Since rate in mph $= \frac{\text{distance in miles}}{\text{time in hours}}$, Tessa's speed on the way to the lake and back home in mph can be expressed as $\frac{d}{1.25}$ and $\frac{d}{0.75}$, respectively, when d is the distance between Tessa's house and the lake. Since she rode 4 mph faster on her way home:

$$\frac{d}{0.75} - \frac{d}{1.25} = 4$$
$$\frac{d}{0.75} \times \frac{4}{4} - \frac{d}{1.25} \times \frac{4}{4} = 4$$
$$\frac{4d}{3} - \frac{4d}{5} = 4$$
$$15\left(\frac{4d}{3} - \frac{4d}{5}\right) = 4(15)$$
$$20d - 12d = 60$$
$$d = 7.5$$

Since the distance between Tessa's house and the lake is 7.5 miles, she rode a total distance of 15 miles in 2 hours (1 hour 15 minutes + 45 minutes = 2 hours). Therefore, her average speed was $\frac{15 \text{ miles}}{2 \text{ hours}} = 7.5$ mph.

96. B: Use trigonometric identities to simplify. First, convert $\sec\theta$ to $\frac{1}{\cos\theta}$.

$$\sin\theta\sec\theta$$

$$\sin\theta \times \frac{1}{\cos\theta}$$

Then, multiply the two values.

$$\frac{\sin\theta}{\cos\theta}$$

Remember, $\frac{\sin\theta}{\cos\theta} = \tan\theta$, so the simplified form of the expression is $\tan\theta$.

97. C: Sketch a diagram (this one is not to scale) and label the known segments. Because $\overline{CD}$ is bisected, the point of tangency divides the segment into two pieces measuring 4 and 4. From here, use the property that two segments are congruent when they originate from the same point outside of a circle and are both tangent to the circle. The point of tangency of $\overline{BC}$ divides the segment into two pieces measuring 4 and 6; the point of tangency of $\overline{AB}$ divides the segment into two pieces measuring 6 and 8; the point of tangency of $\overline{AD}$ divides the segment into two pieces measuring 8 and 4. Therefore $\overline{AD} = 8 + 4 = 12$.

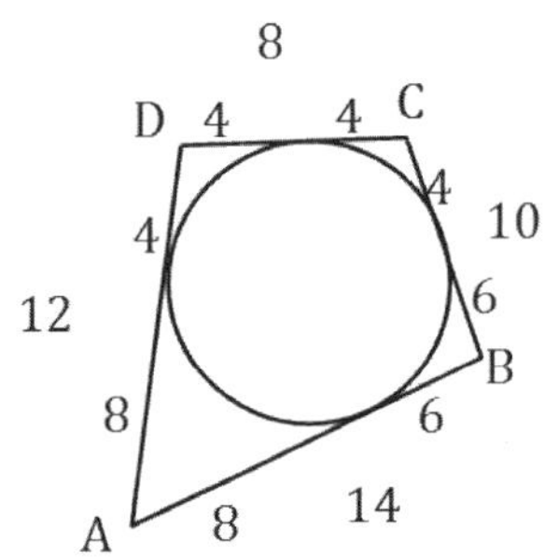

98. A: Below is the graph of $g(x)$.

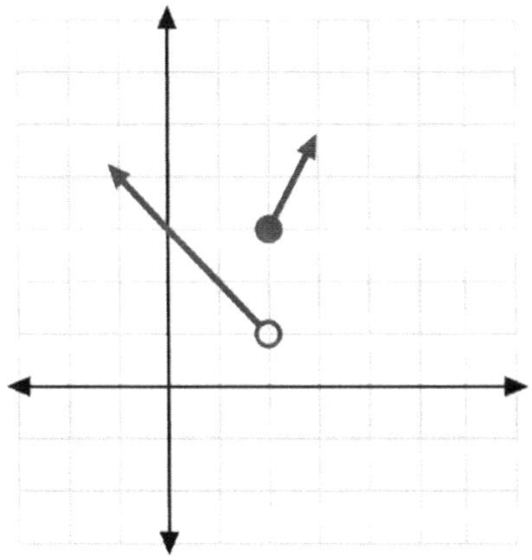

Statement II is true. The graph is discontinuous at $x = 2$. Statement I is false, because $g(3) = 2(3) - 1 = 5$. Statement III is also false because, from the graph, the range of the function is $y > 1$.

99. A: One way to determine which is the graph of $f(x) = -3|-x + 2| + 1$ is to find $f(x)$ for a few values of x. For example, when $x = 0$, $f(0) = -3|0 + 2| + 1 = -5$. Graphs A and C pass through $(0, -5)$, but graphs B and D do not. When $x = 2$, $f(2) = -3|-2 + 2| + 1 = 1$. Graph A passes through (2,1), but graph C does not. Graph A is the correct graph.

100. C: Leonhard Euler made many important contributions to the field of mathematics. One such contribution, Euler's formula $e^{i\varphi} = \cos\varphi + i\sin\varphi = 0$, can be written as $e^{i\pi} + 1 = 0$ when $\varphi = \pi$.